LIBERAL ARTS POWER!

How to Sell It on Your Résumé

Burton Jay Nadler

Peterson's Guides
Princeton, New Jersey

Library of Congress Cataloging in Publication Data

Nadler, Burton Jay, 1953–
    Liberal arts power!

    1. Résumés (Employment) 2. Education,
Humanistic. I. Title.
HF5383.N3   1985   650.1'4   83-22116
ISBN 0-87866-254-5

Printed in the United States of America

10 9 8 7 6 5 4 3 2 1

For information about other Peterson's publications,
please see the listing at the back of this volume.

CONTENTS

Acknowledgments   vii

Introduction   1

The Liberal Arts Graduate and
    the Job Search   5

Steps to Writing Your Résumé:
    A Quick Overview   11

The Chronological Flowchart   13

The Skills Flowchart   20

The Job Target Chart   24

Sample Résumés   32

Writing Your Résumé   87
    The Contents   87
    Résumé Formats   92
    Writing Your Rough Draft   95

Production Techniques   102

Covering Letters   108

A Bibliography for Liberal
    Arts Majors   117

Acknowledgments

This book is dedicated to a number of very special people:

To all of the students who asked "Do you have a few minutes to look at my résumé?"
Each minute spent critiquing your résumés contributed to an ever-increasing understanding of the résumé-writing and job-search processes. With this book I am now able to share with others what you have taught me.

To Terry.
You took a chance and hired someone whose résumé reflected limited experience and you showed me that career planning and placement is a career field with numerous rewards.

To Teri.
We have shared several job searches, each of which resulted in success and in continued professional development. You are proof that a liberal arts job seeker can be successful at whatever she does.

To Jordan.
Your résumé is very, very brief right now. I can't wait to see the entries that the future will bring.

I also want to offer a special word of thanks to the following individuals: Grant Bogle of American Critical Care; Russ Dunham of Procter & Gamble; Kevin Kruse of Bamberger's Department Stores; Tim Plunkett of G. Fox & Co.; Robert Smith of New England Telephone; K. Vinton Taylor of Time Inc.; and Lisa Bowers White of First National Bank of Chicago. These recruiting professionals reviewed many of the sample résumés that appear in this book, offering some very constructive feedback, and provided their own basic views about hiring liberal arts graduates. In addition, my thanks go to the above recruiters for hiring many of the liberal arts job seekers I have worked with over the years.

Introduction

It's about time that the myths associated with liberal arts graduates and the job hunt are cleared up once and for all!

Over the past decade, students, parents, career counselors, and placement professionals have all heard a good bit about the so-called "plight of the liberal arts graduate." Newspaper and magazine articles and television and radio reports have made much of the "fact" that liberal arts students are growing less and less marketable, that they are all having greater and greater difficulty securing employment after graduation. Well, it's about time that the myths associated with liberal arts graduates and the job hunt are cleared up once and for all!

My experience has shown me that liberal arts job seekers may have difficulty getting started, but that once they are armed with the right job-search tools, an understanding of how to implement an effective job-search campaign, and the positive attitudes required for success in any endeavor, they have no trouble finding and keeping excellent jobs. Liberal arts graduates have the qualifications employers seek, and whether they know it or not, they all have the capacity to market these qualifications successfully.

Unfortunately, however, many talented people begin their job search filled with self-doubt and anxiety. Having heard too many horror stories about the "unemployable" liberal arts graduate, they too often come to believe that they have no marketable skills to offer an employer and that their credentials are not strong enough for them to be able to carry out a winning job search. The simple truth is that far too many liberal arts graduates are victims of a self-fulfilling prophecy. Fearing the future and not really expecting to be successful, they make timid and ineffective efforts at finding a job. Because they make such a poor start, they often do encounter difficulty, and too many end up either unemployed or, what may be worse, underemployed, having settled for jobs beneath their capacities.

Liberal arts graduates have proven that they can find jobs that are just as challenging and rewarding as the work secured by their peers who majored in other disciplines. It is true that if one looks at broad statistics, such as the number of recruiting organizations that request interviews with liberal arts graduates or the average salary offers for liberal arts graduates, it is easy to be pessimistic. But if one looks at each liberal arts job seeker as a person who is capable of finding satisfying employment, the real picture begins to emerge.

It is the job seeker who must present himself or herself as being qualified for a particular position; the degree and the major are relatively unimportant.

Unlike students in preprofessional or vocational programs, liberal arts majors generally need to go through a process of self-assessment before they can become really effective job seekers, and they must research careers in order to identify goals. Once they are focused, however, and once they are armed with an effective résumé and the positive attitude required for success, liberal arts graduates have no trouble finding excellent jobs.

In order to succeed in the job search, however, liberal arts students must learn to be self-directed and to implement aggressive job-hunting techniques. They have to adopt a new mind-set. They should not, for example, expect to be recruited directly off the college campus for their first job. Although many students do find employment through the on-campus recruiting system, expecting that this will automatically be the case for most liberal arts job seekers will only serve to perpetuate the previously discussed self-fulfilling prophecy.

Liberal arts job seekers must learn to go directly to employers rather than wait for employers to come to them. These students should certainly participate as much as possible in on-campus recruiting programs, since many large corporations, retailers, banks, consulting firms, and manufacturers do recruit liberal arts graduates, but they should not depend solely on this process to find a job.

It is important to remember that it is the job seeker who must present himself or herself as being qualified for a particular position; the degree and the major are relatively unimportant. Career counselors commonly hear comments like these from liberal arts majors: "I haven't done anything!" ..."What can I put on a résumé?" ..."What can I tell an interviewer?" In most cases, these people are far too critical about their own past, judging important events as "not worth noting on a résumé." It is as if they wish to reject accomplishments as irrelevant before a potential employer has the chance to do so. These individuals have accepted what they have heard and read about liberal arts graduates having little to offer an employer, and, by being overcritical, they are revealing their own anxiety and self-doubt.

In order to write an effective résumé and carry out a successful job search, liberal arts job seekers must at best be confident and self-assured and, at the very least, objective about their abilities and accomplishments. Employers will judge your experiences according to their own criteria, not yours. Your job is to show how your skills and experiences have prepared you for the job. Your job is to sell your "liberal arts power."

If you have done your homework and made the connection between your abilities and the requirements of a particular job, you will feel confident and "liberal arts powerful." Self-criticism and self-doubt recede when you know you have something to offer, when you see your own liberal arts power on your résumé.

This book will show you how to make these connections and how to present them on your résumé. The résumé plays a very important part in the liberal arts graduate's job search. A good résumé will bear a bit of the burden of job hunting for you and it should increase your confidence as well. It will present your liberal arts power on paper and prepare you to present your liberal arts power in person.

The secret to carrying out a successful job search thus lies in the art of marketing oneself and one's skills confidently and with imagination. Liberal arts graduates must develop individualized job-search strategies; they must believe in their abilities to perform tasks associated with the jobs they want; and they must project confidence to all of the employers they communicate with. One of the principal ways of doing all of this—that is, of marketing oneself effectively—is by developing the best résumé possible.

My work as a career counselor at several colleges and universities and in private practice has convinced me that liberal arts graduates have the qualifications employers seek and that they have the capacity to market these qualifications successfully. This has been corroborated by my colleagues in career planning and placement offices across the country. Whether they believe it or not at the outset, liberal arts graduates truly have the power to succeed in the job search and on the job. Once they have taken the time to assess their skills and to tailor their résumés to reflect their own skills and interests, they begin to realize just how powerful they can be. They come to understand that they have their own brand of marketing power—their "liberal arts power"—and that it can be used just as effectively as the credentials presented by graduates of preprofessional or vocational programs.

This book is meant to educate and to motivate. The sample résumés and accompanying analyses will show you what is required to develop an effective résumé of your own. The information and advice offered throughout the book will help you overcome the psychological barriers that may be stopping you from writing a résumé and pursuing a successful job search. This book can be used by first-time job seekers as well as by those who are seeking career changes and new jobs.

Liberal arts graduates have the qualifications employers seek and the capacity to market these qualifications successfully.

3

This book will help you overcome the psychological barriers that may be stopping you from writing a résumé and pursuing a successful job search.

It is my hope that this book and the combined job-search success stories of its readers will begin to counteract the myth of the unemployability of the liberal arts graduate. Self-perpetuating negativism has hurt too many people and hindered too many job searches. It is now time to create realistic and positive attitudes and to write about success stories rather than horror stories. By starting to read this book, you have begun to write your own success story.

The Liberal Arts Graduate and the Job Search

Today's liberal arts job seekers need a new conceptual orientation—they need to learn to think and speak with a "skills vocabulary."

For the purpose of this book, let us return to the original meaning of *artes liberales*—"work befitting a free man." This book is intended to help liberal arts graduates find satisfying work. Because they are truly free to enter any one of numerous career fields, liberal arts graduates must make careful decisions about career goals and adopt special job-hunting strategies. By coming to terms with the job-search process and devising a creative and well-written résumé, all liberal arts graduates can realize the goals of a liberal education—ongoing self-expression and self-fulfillment.

The liberal arts job seeker does in fact bear a greater burden of communicating career goals and qualifications than the graduate of a vocationally oriented curriculum. In most cases, the person's degree title, whether it is a bachelor's, master's, or doctoral degree, does not communicate to the potential employer what the liberal arts graduate truly has to offer, and neither does his or her major.

Too many liberal arts students ask the question: "What can I do with a major in 'X'?" These students are, unfortunately, all laboring under the common misconception that a person's major somehow determines the types of jobs he or she is qualified for. This is simply not true. A major does not equate with a job or a set of jobs, and no one major, whether liberal arts, technical, or business, guarantees that a person will obtain a job. Employers judge candidates according to the skills they possess and their potential ability to perform functions associated with particular job titles and descriptions. Some employers state desired degrees and majors when posting jobs or when recruiting on college campuses, but liberal arts graduates who understand the job-search process know that what is most important is having the required skills and taking the steps necessary to present themselves as qualified candidates. Today's liberal arts job seekers need a new conceptual orientation—they need to learn to think and speak with a "skills vocabulary."

Whether you are a soon-to-be or a recent college graduate looking for your first job, a person seeking new challenges and rewards in a second or third job, someone wishing to change careers or re-enter the work force after spending time at home, or a person who has been forced by circumstances beyond your control to look for a new job, you must understand the hiring process. If you are aware of what the person responsible for hiring does, you will understand what you must do to be successful and why the burden of proving that you are qualified for employment rests on you and not on the title of your major.

The Hiring Process

To fill a particular job, a company establishes a set of qualifications it feels are desirable. Once these skills, areas of knowledge, characteristics, interests, and values are established, the company's hirer—recruiter—searches for candidates who possess them. In some cases, these qualifications are specified in job descriptions, sign-up schedules for on-campus interviews, and want ads. In all cases, the person doing the hiring keeps them clearly in mind.

The hirer reviews résumés and covering letters and interviews candidates for the available position. During interviews, the employer listens for statements about a job seeker's past experiences that reveal whether he or she has the skills and other qualifications being sought. Job seekers who possess these requirements are granted consideration, and eventually one candidate is offered the job.

Well, this seems quite simple. It is, in fact, but that does not mean that job hunting is easy. Looking for a job requires a great deal of work—it is actually one of the most physically and psychologically demanding efforts you will undertake. And although writing a good résumé is one of the most important steps in the process, it is not the only step. You must be prepared to use your résumé effectively and ride the emotional roller coaster of the job search—in some cases for several months—until you find the job that is right for you. Your search will be successful if you keep in mind not only how hiring is done but also how you, the liberal arts job seeker, can best represent yourself to potential employers.

There is NO Excuse for Not Writing Your Résumé Now!

For too many people, writing a résumé is a difficult, anxiety-provoking process that delays rather than advances their job search. Why does the idea of

> **The burden of proving that you are qualified for employment rests on you, not on the title of your major.**

writing a résumé fill people's minds with negative thoughts and apprehensions? To this question, I have frequently heard such answers as these:

"Because writing a résumé is like studying for and taking a final exam. You really don't know what a professor is going to ask on the exam, nor do you know what an employer really wants to see on the résumé. You put in so much time and effort, and it's scary to work so hard and not know what the results might be."

"Because I don't know how to write a résumé. I have heard so many different things about résumés that I am confused. My dad tells me one thing and the counselor at the placement office tells me another. Books on résumé writing present such contradictory information that I don't know what to do. I'm afraid if I don't do it the right way, I'll be wasting my time and jeopardizing my chances of finding a good job."

"Because I don't have anything to put on a résumé. I haven't done very much. I'm not the president of any organization, and I haven't received any academic honors or awards. My work experience is not extensive. Nothing I put on a résumé will impress an employer, so why write one?"

"Because it is hard for me to write about myself. I can't lie about what I have done, and I have never been very good about bragging, making something very ordinary appear special. If that's what I have to do to write a résumé, I would rather not write one."

"Because writing a résumé means that I will have to start looking for a job, and I am afraid of the pressures of a job search. I'd rather wait until I'm better prepared to face the task ahead."

My response to these statements is as follows:

You may not know now what an employer wants to see on a résumé, but after a thorough self-assessment and exploration of careers, you will know what you want to say on your résumé. Knowing the skills you possess and the functions involved in various jobs will enable you to define your employment goals and thus direct the content of your résumé toward a particular field or job.

There is no one right way to write a résumé. Résumé writing is an art, not an exact science. You should therefore feel confident that you can develop a résumé that is right for you, one that fits your own background and goals.

Everyone has something to put on a résumé. You may be judging your past experiences too harshly, or you may not have thoroughly reviewed your accomplishments and achievements. When you have assessed your skills and researched

Résumé writing is an art, not an exact science. You should feel confident that you can develop a résumé that fits your own background and goals.

Employers are impressed not only by what you have done but also by the way you communicate your goals and abilities.

career options, you will be prepared to develop a résumé that presents you as a person qualified for the job you seek. And remember, employers will be impressed not only by what you have done but also by the way you communicate your goals and abilities.

You don't have to brag or lie on a résumé, but you should describe your experiences and abilities as positively as possible. Résumé writing and job hunting are among those experiences that make it appropriate to involve yourself in personal promotion. Résumés are positive documents, and employers want to see what you have done. You can objectively state the facts to an employer without any sleight of hand.

Résumé writing should be viewed as a very exciting activity—one of the first steps on a journey that will end in your finding a challenging and rewarding job. The journey may not be easy, and it may take longer than you would like, but it will end in success. The longer you wait, the more anxious you will get, and the longer it will take before you have that wonderful experience of saying yes to a job offer.

Using Your Résumé

Like the suit of clothes worn to an employment interview, your résumé must project a positive image, and it must fit both you and the circumstances. If you are not comfortable with your résumé—if you don't feel that it is the very best résumé you can use—then you will not be an effective job seeker. This book enables you to try on various résumé styles, and it provides the information you need to create the best résumé you can. You will of course continue to grow intellectually, emotionally, and experientially, and a résumé that fits today may not do so next year, next month, or even next week, so you should always be prepared to change your résumé as needed. After reading this book you will have enough confidence in your résumé to be an effective job seeker, and enough confidence in your résumé-writing skills to change your résumé when necessary.

The résumé is a job-hunting tool. It does not get you a job; rather, it is a tool for you to use to get an interview and for you to use during the interview and follow-up stages of the job search. There are a number of important ways in which you can use your résumé effectively in order to become a successful liberal arts job seeker. As you develop your résumé, you should keep in mind its functions, which are described on the following page.

YOU CAN USE YOUR RÉSUMÉ

- **To initiate contact with a potential employer:**
Accompanied by a covering letter, the résumé will serve in many cases as the initial contact with a prospective employer. Because it is the first indication an employer will have of the type of work you are capable of doing, your résumé must create a positive first impression.

- **To provide a potential employer with a concise summary of education, experience, skills, and goals:**
The résumé is a device for imparting information—information concerning education, employment, extracurricular activities, and any other experiences that have contributed to the development of skills that qualify you for positions you want. You should do this as succinctly as possible, but without omitting information that projects qualifications to an employer. Your résumé should be the best representation of *all* that you have to offer. It should not be limited to an arbitrary page length, but it should be as brief as possible.

- **To facilitate the employment interview by serving as a guide for both interviewer and interviewee:**
The résumé provides a common base of knowledge shared by you and the interviewer and can be used as a map to guide both of you through the two-way street that is the employment interview. The interviewer will ask you to elaborate upon information presented on the résumé. You, in turn, can refer to it in order to cite examples of specific skills that are of interest to the employer. The better the résumé, the more you can use it to ensure a successful interview.

- **To share information with persons assisting in the job search:**
The résumé is an excellent way to inform others of your job search and solicit their help. You can use the résumé to develop and maintain a contact network—a group of resource persons and references. Give copies of your résumé to your contacts and ask them to distribute them as they learn about employment opportunities. Career counselors and others who provide assistance and information can use the résumé to stay informed of your goals and qualifications. People who write letters of recommendation for you can refer to the résumé in order to remind themselves of your specific qualities and accomplishments.

- **To serve as a record to leave with a potential employer or resource person, so follow-up can be done effectively:**
The résumé is your calling card. You can leave it with prospective employers and resource persons to facilitate future communications. You can follow up your résumé with phone calls, letters, or visits and be confident that the recipient of the résumé knows something about your background and goals. Most job offers are made during follow-up contacts.

- **To supplement information given when completing applications:**
Most application forms request a great deal of information yet provide very little space in which to write. Whether you are applying for employment, admission to graduate or professional school, or membership in a professional organization, you can make sure that you are providing all the information required for a thorough consideration of your candidacy by attaching your résumé to the application.

The following sections of this book show you how to write a résumé that can be used for all of the job-hunting activities outlined on page 9. Just remember that the résumé is a tool and keep in mind as you proceed that there are many ways in which you can use it to be successful.

Steps to Writing Your Résumé: A Quick Overview

Working through these exercises will help you answer the questions "What do I have to offer an employer?" and "What kind of résumé is best for me?"

The steps described below have been developed to help you think about your skills and write your résumé in a systematic fashion. The first three steps involve reviewing and documenting your past accomplishments and identifying potential job-search targets. These exercises will help you answer the questions "What do I have to offer an employer?" "What can I put on my résumé?" and "What specific jobs should I keep in mind when writing my résumé?" Working through Steps 4 and 5 will help you find answers to the questions "What kind of résumé is best for me?" "Should I write more than one résumé?" and "How do I go about writing my résumé and having it printed and duplicated?" Numerous liberal arts job seekers have used this method with very positive results, creating résumés that turned out to be very effective tools and that helped them land the jobs they wanted.

Each step is accompanied by exercises and examples that illustrate the actions you must take to complete the step. In addition, target time frames are given for each step. These are meant to provide you with some idea of how many hours it might take to complete each task and to motivate you to allot yourself the time required to do a good job. Note that the total time suggested for completing your résumé is twelve to twenty-one hours. This does not mean that you should accomplish everything in one day, undertaking a marathon résumé-writing effort. The activities should be completed over at least a few days. There are times in the résumé-writing process when you must stop and think, or simply relax, before continuing with the next step.

Proceed through the steps one by one. You can complete the steps at a more leisurely pace than the one suggested by the target time frames, but you should not procrastinate or get bogged down with trivial details. Managing your time, that is, giving yourself enough time to be successful and not wasting time, is very important. It means organizing your schedule so that you have the time you need to do a careful job.

Use the following summary and target time frames to get an idea of what is involved and to organize yourself. Before you actually begin each step, review the goals so that you are absolutely sure of what you want to accomplish at each stage.

STEPS TO WRITING YOUR RÉSUMÉ: A QUICK OVERVIEW

Step 1   **The Chronological Flowchart**

This exercise helps you to document your educational history, notable achievements and activities, and employment experience. You can then use this information to develop a multipurpose or targeted chronological résumé. This exercise also provides a basis for Step 2, the Skills Flowchart.
Target Time: 2 to 4 hours

Step 2   **The Skills Flowchart**

This exercise guides you in identifying the skills you have developed through the experiences you documented on the Chronological Flowchart—skills that are associated with functioning successfully on the job. Once you have a complete list of your skills, you will be able to focus in more easily on specific job targets. You can use the information presented on your Skills Flowchart to create a functional or combination résumé.
Target Time: 2 to 4 hours

Step 3   **The Job Target Chart**

After completing this step you should be better able to identify the jobs you want to aim for and the skills you have developed that should be presented as qualifications for these jobs. You can use this information to devise targeted résumés and to prepare for employment interviews.
Target Time: 2 to 4 hours

Step 4   **The Review of Sample Résumés**

This step involves examining the sample résumés and accompanying analyses that appear in Part 2 to identify which ones illustrate the kinds of contents and formats that would best serve your purposes. All of the résumés were written by liberal arts job seekers, and they include résumés of homemakers who are "returning" to work as well as people who are moving from one job or career field to another. The samples represent many different styles of résumés, and the analyses explain why each liberal arts job hunter developed a particular résumé. Instructions on how to use the samples to develop a rough draft of your résumé are given as well.
Target Time: 2 to 3 hours

Step 5   **Writing Your Résumé**

This is a process that takes you through several revisions from a rough draft to a final version of your résumé. Guidelines for critiquing your drafts are presented.
Target Time: 4 to 6 hours

The Chronological Flowchart

The Chronological Flowchart enables you to identify and document your experiences and achievements in a systematic fashion.

The Chronological Flowchart is a document on which you record your educational and employment experiences and achievements in the order of their occurrence. This document will enable you to identify your skills and, ultimately, to write your résumé.

Use the model that appears on pages 15 to 19 to prepare your own Chronological Flowchart. Before you begin, however, let's take a look at the individual components of the chart.

Dates. Record these in the left-hand margin. Start with the present, noting year and month, academic year, or season, and proceed in reverse chronological order, going as far back as you desire.

Educational History. Describe your graduate, undergraduate, high school, and other academic experiences. Include special programs such as foreign study programs and field-specific institutes (although these can also appear under the Notable Achievements and Activities heading). Cite institutions, dates attended and/or dates graduated, courses and/or majors, credits received, and as much detailed information as you deem appropriate.

Notable Achievements and Activities. Document extracurricular and community activities, travel experiences, and other achievements, including those that could appear in either of the other columns, that have given you a sense of accomplishment and that you judge to be of particular note. List the experience and describe the circumstances and accomplishments involved.

Employment History. List full-time and part-time jobs, internships, and other work experience. Cite where you worked and titles you held, and describe the nature of your activities. You can record volunteer experiences here or under Notable Achievements and Activities, depending on whether or not you see them as work experience.

Stacey York's Chronological Flowchart is presented to illustrate how your flowchart might look. (Stacey's résumés are included among the samples, on pages 85 and 86.) Study her flowchart carefully to see the kinds of things she included. Do not, however, compare yourself with her. You should not judge the quality of your flowchart, or your past experiences, by comparing them with the experiences of others. You are to use this exercise to simply document your accomplishments, not to judge them!

The more information you have on your chart, the more control you will have over the résumé-writing process.

Start your chart by filling in the dates column, then complete the other sections. There is no limit to the number of pages your chart can be. Be as thorough as possible—not critical. The more information you have on your chart, the easier the subsequent steps will be and the more control you will have over the résumé-writing process. Now is the time to put everything down; later you will be more selective about the information you make use of.

Once you have completed the first draft of your flowchart, put it down for a few hours. Then review what you have written, adding information where you feel the chart is incomplete. You may wish to have a friend, family member, or supervisor review the draft with you. Such people might remember details you have forgotten or overlooked.

When you have completed the Chronological Flowchart you may be tempted to skip the next steps and go on to write a multipurpose chronological résumé. (And this may be the only way to proceed if you must have a résumé quickly for the interview you have scheduled two days from now.) I strongly recommend, however, that you complete the Skills Flowchart and the Job Target Chart so that you will develop more focused objectives and have the option of writing either a functional or a chronological résumé. Do not be too quick to skip steps. The more thoroughly you complete all three steps, the more effective your résumé, or résumés, will be and the more control you will have over the entire job-hunting process.

		NOTABLE ACHIEVEMENTS	
DATES	EDUCATIONAL HISTORY	AND ACTIVITIES	EMPLOYMENT HISTORY

CHRONOLOGICAL FLOWCHART   Stacey York   Page 1

DATES	EDUCATIONAL HISTORY	NOTABLE ACHIEVEMENTS AND ACTIVITIES	EMPLOYMENT HISTORY
SENIOR YEAR 1984–85 Spring Term 1985	STANFORD UNIVERSITY A.B., expected June 1985 Major: English Literature	Graduation!	
Winter Term 1985 Fall Term 1984	Courses: Fables & Fabulists; Graphic Art; English Independent Study	3.2 GPA as of Fall 1984	
		STANFORD WOMEN'S CREW Coxswain Novice Four 1983–present Editor, *STANFORD CREW NOTES* Fall 1983–present Write copy; edit and lay out monthly editions; circulate to appropriate on-campus departments and publications, off-campus publications, and alumni. PANHELLENIC SOCIETY Representative of Alpha Chi Omega Sorority Fall 1984 *STANFORD SPORTS NEWS* *SAN FRANCISCO CHRONICLE* *SAN JOSE MERCURY NEWS* *THE STANFORD DAILY* Fall 1981–present Write various articles on Stanford athletics.	STANFORD SPORTS INFORMATION OFFICE Administrative Intern Spring 1983–present Report on all sports events; manage post-game pressbox operations for football season; write articles on Stanford athletes for press releases and athletic department publications, assist in development of press guides and programs. Football Statistician Fall 1984 and 1983 Compiled statistics; wrote game summaries and weekly reports.
Summer 1984	Term Off		MOBIL OIL CORPORATION Public Relations Intern Summer 1984 Assisted staff writers in research for Mobil's Op Ed advertisements, "Observations" columns, and special publications. Proofread copy and checked facts; replied to reader correspondence; coordinated Mobil's School Visitation Program.

CHRONOLOGICAL FLOWCHART	*Stacey York*		Page 2
DATES	EDUCATIONAL HISTORY	NOTABLE ACHIEVEMENTS AND ACTIVITIES	EMPLOYMENT HISTORY
JUNIOR YEAR 1983–84			
Spring Term 1984	STANFORD IN FRANCE Spring 1984 Studied language and culture while living with French family in Nice, France, and attending the Université de Nice.	Traveled throughout France, Italy, and Germany.	
Winter Term 1984	Courses: Introductory French II, Shakespeare II, Instrument Instruction—Keyboard.	STANFORD ALUMNI CLUB OF NORTHERN NEW JERSEY Student Liaison Officer Spring 1983–Winter 1984 Coordinated activities for prospective Stanford students from northern New Jersey at Alumni Club events in NJ and at Stanford. Represented Stanford at college nights at high schools in NJ. Corresponded with applicants and alumni concerning campus events. Greeted and hosted Alumni Club members, freshmen, and prospective students during visits to campus.	
Fall Term 1983	Introductory French I, Developmental Psychology, Shakespeare I	*THE STANFORD DAILY* Sports Reporter Winter 1982–Fall 1983 Covered various sports events for student newspaper. ALPHA CHI OMEGA SORORITY Rush Cochairwoman Fall 1983 Assisted in planning of all rush functions.	

CHRONOLOGICAL FLOWCHART *Stacey York*

DATES	EDUCATIONAL HISTORY	NOTABLE ACHIEVEMENTS AND ACTIVITIES	EMPLOYMENT HISTORY
Summer Term 1983	Courses: Introduction to the Theater, Contemporary American Fiction, Role of Computer Outside Science, Recent U.S. History		PALO ALTO HILTON INN Hostess and Waitress Summer 1983 part-time
SOPHOMORE YEAR 1982–83			
Spring Term 1983	INDEPENDENT STUDY PROJECT Spring 1983 Surveyed student attitudes concerning Stanford Honor Code. Presented results in videotape presentation to student and faculty groups and to administration. Courses: Policy Studies Independent Study, Introduction to Journalism II, Art—Basic Design		STANFORD SPORTS INFORMATION OFFICE Administrative Intern Spring 1983 Selected as one of three interns from over twenty applicants.
Winter 1983	Term Off		BAMBERGER'S DEPARTMENT STORE Salesperson in "Junior World" Winter 1983 Assisted customers, maintained stock, assisted buyers in selecting merchandise.
Fall Term 1982	SOCIAL PSYCHOLOGY RESEARCH STUDY Fall 1982 Conducted survey of passengers using shuttle-bus system utilizing interviews. Developed questionnaires, collected and analyzed data to determine use patterns and opinions. Results presented to shuttle-bus management. Courses: Social Psychology, Women & Literature, Introduction to Policy Studies		

DATES	EDUCATIONAL HISTORY	NOTABLE ACHIEVEMENTS AND ACTIVITIES	EMPLOYMENT HISTORY
Summer 1982	Term Off		BAMBERGER'S DEPARTMENT STORE Salesperson in "Housewares" Summer 1982 Assisted customers and maintained stock.
FRESHMAN YEAR 1981–82			
Spring Term 1982	Courses: Instrument Instruction—Keyboard, Introduction to Psychology, American Political System	STANFORD ALUMNI CLUB OF NORTHERN NEW JERSEY Student Liaison Officer Spring 1982 Selected as one of two student liaison officers.	
Winter Term 1982	Courses: English Literature—Chaucer to Milton; Calculus and Differential Equations, Introduction to Journalism I		
Fall Term 1981	STANFORD UNIVERSITY Enrolled as freshman Courses: Introduction to Literature and Composition, History of the U.S. 1700–1900, Introduction to Calculus		
Summer 1981			BAMBERGER'S DEPARTMENT STORE Supervisor/Salesperson Fall 1979–Summer 1981 Responsible for salespersons, nightly closing activities, and maintaining departments in managers' absence. Rotated throughout store as needed. Youngest such supervisor in store. Worked evenings, weekends, and holidays.

CHRONOLOGICAL FLOWCHART   *Stacey York*

DATES	EDUCATIONAL HISTORY	NOTABLE ACHIEVEMENTS AND ACTIVITIES	EMPLOYMENT HISTORY
SENIOR YEAR 1980–81	COLUMBIA HIGH SCHOOL Diploma, June 1981 Top 10% of class of 850	NATIONAL HONOR SOCIETY 1980 *THE MIRROR* Senior Yearbook Editor Fall 1980–Spring 1981 Coordinated activities of five editors and twenty-five staff members. Included business and production decisions, layout, copy, advertising, and photography.	
JUNIOR YEAR 1979–80		JUNIOR CLASS SECRETARY Fall 1979–Spring 1980 *THE MIRROR* Yearbook Staff Member Winter 1979–Spring 1980 Wrote pieces, assisted in layout of sports section, and sold ads.	

The Skills Flowchart

In order to be a successful job hunter, you must learn how to translate experiences into skills.

On your Chronological Flowchart, you documented academic, extracurricular, and employment experiences. In order to become a successful job hunter, you must learn how to translate experiences into skills, orienting your thinking and that of employers toward your potential for the successful performance of specific tasks. The following exercise will assist you in identifying the skills and characteristics you have that can be applied to potential job targets. Once you are aware of your skills and how they relate to specific jobs, and have expressed this on your résumé, you will truly have liberal arts power!

The Skills Flowchart is made up of three separate components:

Experience. You can list all of the academic, extracurricular, and employment experiences noted on your Chronological Flowchart or just a few, but the more you include, the more complete your skills analysis will be. You can decide later which skills you would most like to use day after day on the job.

Basic Skills. List all the skills you utilized or developed through each of your academic, extracurricular, and employment experiences. Here you are answering the basic question "What did I do, and what did I learn, in connection with the job, extracurricular activity, or academic experience?" Use the list of functional skills that appears below to help you identify your own.

Accounting/Bookkeeping	Motivating
Analyzing/Evaluating	Organizing/Maintaining Data
Appraising/Estimating	Performing
Arranging/Displaying	Planning
Budgeting	Printing
Calculating	Promoting
Coaching	Providing Medical Treatment
Computing/Data Processing	Reading/Proofreading
Counseling/Advising	Repairing
Constructing	Recruiting
Coordinating	Representing/Buying
Designing	Researching
Directing	Selling/Distributing
Editing	Speaking
Examining	Sketching/Painting/Photographing
Handling Complaints	Teaching
Interpreting/Translating	Tutoring
Interviewing	Using Instruments and Equipment
Managing/Supervising	Working in Laboratories
Meeting the Public	Writing

In selecting the skills you want to emphasize on your résumé, give first priority to those you enjoy using.

Of course, you don't have to limit yourself to the skills listed above. Be creative and open-minded when citing skills associated with your experiences. Think of what you did beyond the job description. For example, you might have been hired as a file clerk, but if you *reorganized* the filing system, you did more than merely *file*. Note as many skills as you like. Use descriptive phrases if necessary to describe a skill.

Skills Headings. Next take stock of the various skills you cited in the Basic Skills column and group them into a number of broad working categories, using such general headings as "writing," "managing," and "performing." In selecting the skills you want to emphasize on your résumé, give first priority to those you enjoy using and second priority to those you think you are best at. Document your experiences under each skills heading, noting where you exercised or developed that skill.

The Skills Flowchart on pages 22 and 23 is that of Stacey York, the same liberal arts job seeker whose Chronological Flowchart you have studied. By studying Stacey's Chronological and Skills flowcharts you will understand the relationship between these two documents and the two exercises that produced them. You may also wish to review Stacey's chronological and functional résumés, which appear on pages 85 and 86, respectively, to see how the two flowcharts influenced the final products.

You can now complete your own Skills Flowchart. Start by listing experiences from your Chronological Flowchart, then complete the other sections. As before, be thorough and list as many experiences as you wish. There is no limit to the number of entries. Again, the more information you have on your chart, the more control you will have over the résumé-writing process.

Once you have completed the first draft of your Skills Flowchart, put it down for a few hours. Then review it and add to it where the information seems incomplete. As you did with the Chronological Flowchart, you may wish to have someone who knows you well review the draft with you.

You should spend time thinking hard about the Skills Headings section of the flowchart. When revising your initial draft, add more skills and elaborate upon the situations in which you developed and utilized your skills.

Once you have completed the Chronological and Skills flowcharts you can write a multipurpose functional résumé. But, again, I strongly recommend that you complete Step 3, the Job Target Chart, so that you don't deprive yourself of the option of creating a targeted résumé.

SKILLS FLOWCHART **Stacey York**		Page 1

EXPERIENCE	BASIC SKILLS	SKILLS HEADINGS
STANFORD WOMEN'S CREW	Coxswain: motivating, organizing, disciplining. Editor, *STANFORD CREW NOTES*: writing, editing, layout, circulating, promoting.	Note: Create Skills Headings by grouping the information listed under Basic Skills into several broad working categories. You can then use these general headings to organize information about your skills and experiences on your résumé.
PANHELLENIC SOCIETY	Representative: analyzing, organizing, planning, leading, decision making.	• WRITING—journalistic and expository, through course work in English and journalism and experiences with *Stanford Daily*, *Crew Notes*, Sports Information Office, and *The Mirror*.
STANFORD SPORTS NEWS *SAN FRANCISCO CHRONICLE* *SAN JOSE MERCURY NEWS* *THE STANFORD DAILY*	Reporter: writing, reporting, interviewing, researching.	• EDITING—knowledge of grammar and of editing through course work in English and journalism and experiences with *Stanford Daily*, *Crew Notes*, Sports Information Office, Mobil, and *The Mirror*.
STANFORD SPORTS INFORMATION OFFICE	Administrative Intern: writing, editing, layout, public relations, promoting. Football Statistician: calculating, analyzing, writing.	• LAYOUT AND DESIGN—knowledge of layout and design from courses in journalism and art, experiences with *Crew Notes*, Sports Information Office, *The Mirror*, and an interest in oil and acrylic painting. Also photography.
MOBIL OIL CORPORATION	Public Relations Intern: researching, proofreading, organizing, corresponding.	
STANFORD IN FRANCE	Traveling, learning foreign language, understanding and adapting to foreign culture, interpreting and translating.	• RESEARCHING—learned how to develop and implement research designs by working on honor code and shuttle-bus surveys. Did research for Sports Information Office, for Mobil, and for all reporting positions.
STANFORD ALUMNI CLUB OF NORTHERN NEW JERSEY	Student Liaison Officer: organizing, representing, recruiting, promoting, public relations, corresponding.	• ORGANIZING AND MANAGING—learned how to manage tasks and people and analyze data through experiences with Bamberger's, Mobil, Sports Information Office, and Alpha Chi Omega Sorority.
STANFORD DAILY	Reporter: writing, reporting, interviewing, researching.	
ALPHA CHI OMEGA SORORITY	Rush Cochairwoman: organizing, promoting, motivating, planning.	• PERFORMING AND CREATING—knowledge of theatre gained by taking courses and working on high school productions. Capable of making presentations and performing before groups. Play piano and organ; paint in watercolors.
INDEPENDENT STUDY PROJECT FOR POLICY STUDIES	Researching, developing surveys, interviewing, analyzing data, producing videotape presentation.	
SOCIAL PSYCHOLOGY RESEARCH STUDY	Researching, developing attitude assessment procedures, interviewing, analyzing data.	

SKILLS FLOWCHART *Stacey York*

EXPERIENCE	BASIC SKILLS	SKILLS HEADINGS
PALO ALTO HILTON	Hostess and Waitress: dealing with public, handling complaints, serving public, using physical stamina on the job.	Note: Create Skills Headings by grouping the information listed under Basic Skills into several broad working categories. You can then use these general headings to organize information about your skills and experiences on your résumé.
BAMBERGER'S DEPARTMENT STORE	Salesperson: selling, buying, organizing, arranging, displaying.	• PUBLIC RELATIONS AND SELLING—able to promote image and sell products (Stanford Alumni Club of Northern New Jersey, Bamberger's, Alpha Chi Omega Sorority, and high school yearbook experiences).
	Supervisor: supervising, organizing, motivating, selling, buying, arranging, displaying, accounting.	
ENGLISH LITERATURE MAJOR AND JOURNALISM CLASSES	Reading, writing, reporting, judging relative merits of written works, knowledge of grammar.	• FOREIGN LANGUAGE AND CULTURE— knowledge of foreign cultures gained through travel experiences and foreign study; conversant in French.
INSTRUMENTAL INSTRUCTION AND ART CLASSES	Piano playing, sketching, painting, performing.	
THE MIRROR—HIGH SCHOOL YEARBOOK	Senior Editor: editing, writing, layout, managing, delegating, motivating, photography, selling.	
	Staffer: writing, layout, photography, selling.	

The Job Target Chart

Your choice of jobs will be limited only by a lack of awareness of the skills you possess and ignorance of the opportunities that exist.

As I said at the beginning of this book, it is extremely important for you to realize that your major in college does not limit your career opportunities. Your choice of jobs will be limited only by a lack of awareness of the skills you possess and ignorance of the opportunities that exist.

Once you have identified your skills and researched the functions involved in various jobs and careers, you will know what jobs you most want to seek and you will be able to write a targeted résumé. As I have said before, a targeted résumé can be an especially effective tool for the liberal arts job seeker who wants to present himself or herself not simply as a major, but as an individual qualified to perform on the job. The objective you state on your résumé is a handle you can hold on to and a handle you can present to potential employers so they can grasp what you are looking for and the qualifications you possess.

Some of you have already undertaken a great deal of research and have very focused objectives in mind. If you feel you have enough information, you can go ahead and complete your Job Target Chart. If you do not have goals that you can articulate to employers, you should take a bit of time out for some research. Understanding jobs and careers is essential to developing objectives and selling your liberal arts power, and you should take the time to do the research necessary.

A good way to begin your research is to consult some of the many books that provide information on careers. The bibliography on page 117 describes some of the basic materials you should be aware of.

The information you acquire through reading and informational interviews, added to what you already know about career fields and what you will learn from other sources, will help you focus your thinking and decide on job goals. And once you establish your goals you will be prepared to write an effective résumé and take appropriate action. Remember, the more you know about a career field and your job target, the more likely you will be to receive an offer to work within that field. Liberal arts graduates who have not had course work or experiences that are directly related to a specific industry must show that they are knowledgeable about the jobs they are seeking.

Your Job Target Chart will bring together the information on your Chronological and Skills

INFORMATIONAL INTERVIEWS: AN EFFECTIVE RESEARCH TECHNIQUE

One of the best ways to learn about careers you are interested in is to talk with people working in those fields. Use the contacts you have now—friends, relatives, professors, alumni(ae), and career service professionals—to help you identify likely candidates for such "informational interviews."

• Tips on the informational interview:
Try to conduct your first informational interviews with people you know so you can become polished before you interview strangers.

Be thoroughly prepared. This is your show. You are conducting the interview, so feel free to use a list of prepared questions and to take notes or, if given permission, tape the session.

Always take a résumé with you, even if it is a multipurpose one. You can use it to simply and quickly share information about your background so that you can get to the task of finding out about the interviewee's background more easily.

Stress that you are seeking information only, not a job. You may have to restate this several times. Honesty in this regard is very important. If after an informational interview you decide that you would like to seek employment within the organization of the interviewee, you may send a letter indicating your interest in pursuing employment and requesting information about procedures you should follow. Enclose a résumé with this letter (a résumé that may now have a statement of objective based on what you learned from the informational interview) and follow up with a phone call to discuss appropriate next steps.

Keep an open mind and listen closely to what is being said. Evaluate the source of the information objectively, and get more than one side of a story before deciding to stop researching a potential career or before targeting a specific job.

Always end an informational interview with a referral request, asking about other people to talk to or materials to read. In this way, you will be continually developing a network of contacts and a bibliography of resources.

Always follow up an interview with a thank-you letter. You may use the thank-you letter to request additional information or, as discussed, to ask to be considered for employment.

Questions you may wish to ask:

What are the duties/functions/responsibilities of your job?

What are the educational/training requirements?

What abilities or personal qualities do you believe are most important for this field/job?

Which of my abilities or personal qualities would be important in this field/job? (Ask this if the interviewee knows you well.)

Who is the department head or supervisor for this job? What is his/her title?

How does one enter this field/job? How did you enter it? What are typical entry-level titles and functions?

How did you get to where you are and what are your long-range goals?

Do you have any advice for someone who is trying to get started in this field?

What kind of organizations hire people to perform the functions you do here?

Do you know of other persons I may contact to discuss this career field? Can you suggest materials I should read concerning the field? (A question that should always be asked)

The more people you talk to about your career interests and about your job-search efforts, the more likely you will be to succeed. If you cannot arrange an employment interview with an employer, ask for an informational interview. Keep your lines of communication open.

flowcharts and the results of your research into jobs and careers, showing you how your experiences relate to the jobs you are interested in. Be as thorough as possible. There is no limit to the number of pages your chart should be. Again, the more information you put on the chart, the easier subsequent steps will be.

First review the sample Job Target Chart created by Stacey York, which appears on pages 28 and 29. Then start your own by making several three-column sheets with the headings Field/Job Title, Functional Description, and Relevant Experiences and Skills. Fill in the columns one at a time, in the order they are presented below.

Field/Job Title. List the career fields and job titles that interest you most. Do not be afraid to state specific titles. By doing so you are not "limiting yourself" or "closing any doors," phrases I hear too often from liberal arts job seekers who in fact limit themselves by their lack of focus and who have trouble finding a job because they are unwilling to open doors. You are not accepting a job offer here, but simply stating potential job targets. If you are unable to come up with titles you are interested in, perhaps you should undertake a bit more career research.

Functional Description. For each career field and job you have listed as a potential job target in the first column, describe in concise terms the functions and day-to-day responsibilities. Quantity—the length of your description—is less important than quality. If you have a clear understanding of what is expected of someone who holds a particular job, and if you are able to write accurate descriptions of potential job targets, you are prepared to communicate your goals and qualifications to a potential employer. You are then ready to sell your liberal arts power. If you are unable to articulate your job goals, you must continue your exploration of careers by reading appropriate materials and interviewing people who are knowledgeable.

Relevant Experiences and Skills. In the last column of this chart, you relate the information contained in the previous charts to your job targets. The Chronological Flowchart documents the experiences that have given you opportunities to develop and utilize skills. The Skills Flowchart describes the skills you have developed and used. Now, using your Chronological and Skills flowcharts, cite the experiences and skills that relate to the functions of each job in column 1 (Field/Job Title). As you can see by looking at Stacey York's Job Target Chart, the skills you list in column 3 (Relevant Experiences and

If you have a clear understanding of what is expected of someone who holds a particular job, you will be able to communicate your goals and qualifications to employers.

JOB TARGET CHART Stacey York

FIELD/JOB TITLE	FUNCTIONAL DESCRIPTION	RELEVANT EXPERIENCES AND SKILLS
PRINT & BROADCAST MEDIA—JOURNALISM • Editorial Assistant • Researcher • Reporter	**EDITORIAL ASSISTANT** (working for newspapers, magazines, or book publishers; assisting editors with activities involved in the preparation of copy, photography, illustration and graphics). Develop and assign story ideas; communicate with writers and readers; proof, edit, and rewrite copy; lay out publications; coordinate printing activities; and administer to details involved in all areas of editing and publishing. **RESEARCHER** (working for newspapers or magazines or radio or television stations). Research specific story-related facts to develop story and to check accuracy of story; maintain files on subject areas, including facts and photographs; provide writers and reporters with information as needed; proof, edit, and rewrite copy; locate hard-to-find information when needed. **REPORTER** (working for newspapers or magazines or radio or television stations). Research and write stories. Direct writing and reporting style to particular audience.	**EXPERIENCES** • *Stanford Daily* • *Crew Notes* • Sports Information Office • Mobil Corporation • English and Journalism Courses • Free-Lance Articles • *The Mirror* **SKILLS** • Writing • Editing • Layout and Design • Researching • Organizing and Managing • Performing
ADVERTISING • Account Executive Trainee • Media Planner • Marketing Researcher	**ACCOUNT EXECUTIVE TRAINEE** (working for advertising agencies as a trainee, as an entry-level employee in medial planning or marketing research, or as an assistant account executive). Account executives coordinate all who work on the ad campaign, interacting with client and agency personnel. Account executives utilize marketing and financial analysis skills to make decisions concerning ad campaigns. **ENTRY-LEVEL MEDIA PLANNER** (determining which types of media are most cost-effective for meeting desired goals of ad campaigns and undertaking administrative tasks associated with purchasing advertising time or space). Media planners use quantitative abilities to determine appropriate media for campaign and to write contracts. Media planners must learn about various types of media, their costs, and their influence on target markets and maintain awareness of changing media trends. **MARKETING RESEARCHER** (compiling and analyzing data to plan campaigns). Marketing researchers also develop and administer surveys, conduct market group discussions, and utilize data-collection techniques to analyze motivation and buying behavior and to determine effectiveness of campaigns.	**EXPERIENCES** • Sports Information Office • Independent Study Project • Social Psychology Research Project • Alpha Chi Omega Sorority • Stanford Alumni Club of Northern New Jersey • Bamberger's Department Store Note: It may become obvious when a list of experiences becomes rather long that you are *very* qualified for a particular job and that a functional or combination résumé, highlighting skills associated with the experiences, would be effective. **SKILLS** • Organizing and Managing • Researching • Layout and Design • Public Relations and Selling • Creating

FIELD/JOB TITLE	FUNCTIONAL DESCRIPTION	RELEVANT EXPERIENCES AND SKILLS
CONSULTING • Research Assistant or Associate	**RESEARCH ASSISTANT/ASSOCIATE** (working for general management, strategic planning, or specialized consulting firms). Research may involve large industry overviews or specialized analyses concerning particular issues. Information gathered is used by consultants to determine possible solution to clients' problems and to develop reports and presentations to make to clients.	**EXPERIENCES** • Independent Study Project • Social Psychology Research Project • English Literature Major • Psychology Minor **SKILLS** • Researching • Writing • Organizing and Managing
POLITICS • Aide for candidate or office holder	**POLITICAL AIDE.** This work involves assisting in campaign efforts or in daily operations of offices; coordinating volunteers; arranging for press coverage of events; acting as an advance person to coordinate all aspects of visit or event; and researching possible policy position papers. Operations work involves communicating with constituents; researching potential legislation and related issues; developing draft legislation and policy statements; and writing press releases for office holder.	**EXPERIENCES** • Stanford Alumni Club of Northern New Jersey • Independent Study Project • Social Psychology Research Project • Bamberger's Department Store • Alpha Chi Omega Sorority • Panhellenic Society • Stanford Sports Information Office • English Literature Major • Psychology Minor **SKILLS** • Organizing and Managing • Public Relations and Selling • Researching • Writing

Understanding job requirements and being able to make the connection between what the job demands and what you can offer is crucial to success in the job hunt.

Skills) should be the kind you identified in column 2 (Functional Description) as being relevant to your job targets.

In the process of matching up your skills and specific job functions, you may find that you need to rewrite your brief descriptions of your experiences and abilities in order to tailor them to your job targets. This is where "selling yourself" comes in. *The more you can make your qualifications fit the job description, the more qualified for the job you can appear!* I am not talking about distorting the truth or making up false information. I am saying that you need to know about specific job requirements and you need to be able to show how your skills and knowledge are appropriate for jobs you are interested in. This is crucial to success in your job hunt. It is not puffing up your credentials or proving that you're the best. It is simply making the connection between what you can offer and what the job demands. Making this connection between your past and present self and your future working self through research, analysis, and imagination is what liberal arts power is all about.

Once you have completed the first draft of your Job Target Chart, put it down for at least a few hours. Then review it to see whether you need to add information to it; you may see that you don't have enough information about a particular career and that you need to do additional research. You may wish to have a career counselor, friend, family member, or someone working in a career field of interest (perhaps someone you have interviewed for information) review the draft with you. His or her reactions could be very valuable. You may also want to actually draw up your résumé before undertaking additional research. Knowing where you are going—what your résumé might look like and how you might use it as part of an effective job-hunting campaign—could provide necessary direction to your research.

Remember, be thorough! It may take more than one draft to complete the exercise. Do not be afraid to take some time out to continue exploring careers before you go on to the next résumé-writing steps. After completing the final draft of your Job Target Chart, pick the three job titles from the Field/Job Title column that are of most interest to you. You may use these three potential job targets as objectives on three separately targeted résumés or, if they are related to each other, incorporate them on a single targeted résumé. The limit of three does not mean that you cannot look for jobs other than those listed, but it does help you set priorities and cope with a manageable number of goals.

Having completed the first three of the five steps outlined on page 12, you are now prepared to write a multipurpose or targeted résumé, using either a functional or chronological format. You can now move on to the final steps, which involve reviewing samples and analyses, writing drafts and a final version, and printing and duplication.

Keep in mind that you can go back and revise your charts or begin anew at any time. Remember, your first résumé will not be your last. These exercises can help you to prepare for employment interviews.

READ ON ... IDENTIFY RÉSUMÉS
THAT CAN BE USED FOR YOUR
PURPOSES ... PUT YOUR LIBERAL
ARTS POWER ON PAPER ... WRITE AN
EFFECTIVE RÉSUMÉ AND SUCCEED!!

Sample Résumés

Now that you have established potential job targets, you are prepared to undertake the next step toward completion of your résumé: the review of sample résumés and identification of styles and formats that best serve your purposes. The sample résumés presented for your review were written by liberal arts graduates with a variety of backgrounds and career goals, and they illustrate different formats and duplication techniques. The three most basic formats—chronological, functional, and combination—are represented.

To review: The chronological résumé is the most traditional format, with information presented under major headings in reverse chronological order. The functional résumé is skills-oriented, presenting information under skills headings and describing experiences in terms of the functions performed. The combination résumé is a blend of these formats. Some of the résumés were written with a specific job objective in mind, while others were developed to be used for exploring a variety of career possibilities.

Each sample résumé is accompanied by a discussion of the résumé writer's particular situation and reasons for using a certain approach. These analyses give you an insider's perspective, showing you the problems liberal arts résumé writers confront and the way they can solve them by using creative formats, graphics, and copying techniques.

To determine which liberal arts job seekers share background characteristics—majors, extracurriculars, work experiences—with you, ask yourself the following questions after you have completed your first perusal of the samples and analyses:

Which résumés state career goals that are of interest to me?

Which résumés contain descriptions of academic, extracurricular, and work experiences that seem to parallel mine?

Which résumés do I find most attractive and why?

Which design and duplication techniques seem most effective?

Which formats would be most appropriate for my purposes?

Study the sample résumés to identify styles and formats that can best serve your needs.

The résumés presented here document real academic, extracurricular, and work experiences. Use these samples to learn about creative approaches to résumé writing.

Which analyses discuss circumstances similar to my own?

Which résumés are the best models for me?

There is nothing more frustrating for a liberal arts résumé writer than to review sample résumés that seem to be written by super students, résumés that describe accomplishments that seem beyond the capabilities of most students. The résumés presented here document real academic, extracurricular, and work experiences. Although the names of students, schools, and employers have been changed to ensure confidentiality, most of the résumés presented in the following pages are of actual liberal arts job seekers who landed good jobs after graduation. Moreover, most of the sample résumés have been reviewed by employers from different industries to ensure that they reflect the qualities employers seek.

Review the samples and analyses with an open mind. Avoid making statements like "Look at all he has done! I haven't done anything." "She is interested in banking and has worked in a bank for three summers. I don't have any related work experience." "How can I compete with people whose résumés look like this?" The samples are meant to help you write the very best résumé possible, not to frustrate you. They are presented to illustrate various approaches to résumé writing, so do not compare yourself to these liberal arts job seekers. Each job seeker is an individual, and you will be successful with your own background and qualifications.

Jordan Elizabeth Alna:
This Biology Major Means Business

Special Features
- A combination functional and chrono-logical résumé using a Qualifications and Capabilities section
- Creative graphics highlight headings

The Problem. Jordan wanted to stress the fact that she had diverse interests and abilities. She had not only a science major but numerous work and extracurricular experiences as well, and each of these experiences had provided her with skills that she believed could be presented as qualifications to an employer in the business world.

Jordan had at first thought it would be best to use a traditional chronological résumé to present and describe her diverse experiences. After trying this kind of résumé out on several employers without success, however, she was told by a helpful recruiter that even though the word "business" was included in the objective, the résumé gave the impression that Jordan was primarily interested in lab research. This was because she had emphasized her biology training at the beginning of the résumé.

The Solution. After mulling over the recruiter's comments, Jordan thought it might be best to try out a combination functional and chrono-logical résumé. She decided that the first thing she needed to do was specify a narrower job target. After realizing that she was more interested in the health-care industry than in business in general, Jordan chose to focus on jobs in the areas of pharmaceutical sales, health-care administration, and public relations for hospitals or health-care products manufacturers. She then added a Qualifications and Capabilities section, which resulted in a résumé that better matched the skills and interests stated in the objective. Jordan's revised résumé turned out to be much more dynamic in its presentation of the specific skills that can be used on the jobs Jordan thinks she would like.

Special Note. In addition to investigating the options discussed above, Jordan is exploring the possibilities of teaching science courses in a private secondary school or of obtaining a position in a residence life office of a college or university. For these positions, Jordan developed a separate chronological résumé without an objective. For these fields, the more detailed chronological approach was more appropriate.

Format and Layout. Jordan's résumé features very appealing graphics. The spacing is attractive, and the double rules to the left and right of each heading clearly set off one section from another. Jordan also made use of several different type styles and elements to highlight important words—larger type for main headings and italic for degrees and titles.

Summary. Jordan the biology major means business. She first tried out a chronological résumé, believing it would be the most effective type for her to use, but she had the courage to change the résumé to create a better job-search tool. Jordan will be successful. She should have no trouble finding a position in the health-care industry. She has demonstrated her flexibility and her willingness to adapt her job-search tools in order to attract attention from potential employers.

=========== JORDAN ELIZABETH ALNA ===========

Doane Hall, Box A11   34 Glenmere Road
Denison University   Little Rock, Arkansas 72116
Granville, Ohio 43023   501-753-0055
614-587-6276

=========== OBJECTIVE ===========

Opportunity to use organizational and communications skills and scientific background in the health-care industry.

=========== QUALIFICATIONS AND CAPABILITIES ===========

Academic course work in natural sciences provided understanding of scientific method, laboratory experience, and knowledge of theories and applications.

Extracurricular activities and work experiences involved establishment of personal and group goals, development of plans for accomplishing specific tasks, management of procedures and personnel, and use of persuasive skills.

As Hospital Volunteer was exposed to all operations of health-care facility and worked with doctors, nurses, administrators, and volunteers.

As Teaching Assistant developed lesson plans and acted as a liaison between professor and students. Capable of making group presentations and evaluating performance of others.

As Research Assistant followed instructions and worked independently, maintaining accurate records and writing detailed reports. Capable of working without supervision.

As Resident Adviser trained in counseling and program planning. Capable of motivating others to accomplish objectives and dealing with problem situations.

As Management Intern and Office Assistant worked within business settings requiring public relations and organizational abilities. Coordinated activities and interacted with the public. Capable of creating and implementing plans and organizing resources and personnel to meet objectives.

=========== EDUCATION ===========

DENISON UNIVERSITY   Granville, Ohio
Bachelor of Science in Biology   May, 1986

=========== WORK EXPERIENCE ===========

DENISON UNIVERSITY DEPARTMENT OF BIOLOGY   Granville, Ohio
    Teaching Assistant   Fall 1985 and Spring 1986
    Research Assistant   Spring 1985–Spring 1986
DENISON UNIVERSITY OFFICE OF RESIDENCE LIFE   Granville, Ohio
    Resident Adviser   Fall 1984–Spring 1986
DENISON UNIVERSITY OFFICE OF HOUSING AND CONFERENCE COORDINATION   Granville, Ohio
    Management Intern   Summer 1985
    Coordinated conferences and programs. Arranged for facilities and equipment. Planned housing assignments. Represented Denison at social functions. Compiled and analyzed evaluations and wrote report suggesting improvements.
MERRILL LYNCH PIERCE FENNER & SMITH   Little Rock, Arkansas
    Office Assistant   Summer 1984
    Answered customer questions by phone and performed secretarial functions for brokers.

=========== EXTRACURRICULAR ACTIVITIES ===========

KAPPA KAPPA GAMMA SORORITY   Denison University
    Panhellenic Rush Chairperson   Fall 1985–Spring 1986
    Elected to coordinate rush activities of all sororities. Designed and prepared rush booklet. Organized pre-rush activities.
    Member   Spring 1982–Spring 1986
SOPHOMORE ADVISERS   Denison University
    Sophomore Adviser Coordinator   Spring 1983
    Elected to coordinate social functions and promote group unity. Established newsletter. Organized retreat. Represented sophomore advisers to administration.
MEMORIAL HOSPITAL   North Little Rock, Arkansas
    Volunteer   Summers 1982 and 1983

=========== REFERENCES ===========

Available upon request.

Joseph E. Byrne:
An Anthropology Major Discovers the Law

Special Features
- Targeted résumé with skills noted in the statement of objective
- Simple résumé highlighting accomplishments

The Problem. From the day he entered college, Joseph E. Byrne thought that he wanted to pursue a career in retailing someday. He did not know that he would major in anthropology and minor in psychology, nor that he would grow more and more interested in law as a career field as he got closer to graduation. In fact, during his senior year Joe decided that he would postpone his plans for a retailing career in order to explore law-related jobs. "I have so much retail and sales experience, I could always get into retailing if I wanted to," he told himself. He felt that working for a law firm for a year or two would help him decide whether law school was the right next step. After talking to several alumni and to counselors at his college's career planning and placement office, Joe developed a résumé that he could use in his efforts to find such a position. The problem Joe had to overcome was that he had taken no law-related course work and had no law-related work experience.

The Solution. Joe decided that the best way to sell his strengths would be to simply state on the résumé the two most important qualities he possesses that are important in law-related jobs—research and writing skills. He includes these skills in his Objective and supports his claim of possessing them in the discussion of skills that follows.

Joe presents all of his academic and employment experiences in a straightforward and traditional manner, highlighting certain employment accomplishments by indenting the explanations. His résumé thus combines the functional and chronological approaches.

Joe also uses several writing samples as evidence of his skills. He summarizes some of his best research papers and creates a collection of abstracts to distribute to potential employers. These abstracts note the varied research topics Joe undertook while in school and illustrate his writing style. Of course, Joe makes a connection between his academic experiences and the requirements of working for a law firm in his covering letters (see samples beginning on page 114).

Format and Layout. Joe's résumé is traditional in its appearance because most law firms are traditional and somewhat conservative. He wanted to make the very best first impression by using a résumé that is well written and professionally printed.

Summary. Joe discovered late in his academic career that he wanted to explore law as a possible profession, and he has decided to do so by taking a job in the field. This simple yet effective résumé is his first step to success.

Typewritten using a Courier element. ➡

JOSEPH E. BYRNE

Permanent Address   Temporary Address
2 Livingston Avenue   Box 1222
Livingston, NJ 07039   Tulane University
201-740-9841   New Orleans, LA 70118
                                                     504-865-7764

Objective   Position in a law firm utilizing research and writing skills.

Skills   Have initiated and completed numerous research projects. Can
             locate and use reference materials to uncover facts, analyze
             data, and develop written presentations. Capable of writing
             detailed reports and concise, effective synopses.

             Adapt to ever-changing situations and work well under pressure.

Education   **Tulane University, New Orleans, LA**
             Bachelor of Arts, December 1985
             Major: Anthropology   Minor: Psychology

             Additional course work in English, history, earth sciences,
             economics, political science, and public policy.

Honors   Dean's List, Fall 1984 and Spring 1985

Activities   University Residence Council
             Freshman Adviser
             Residence Counselor
             Intramural Athletics

Experience

Summers   Herman's World of Sporting Goods, Livingston, NJ

1984   Salesman

1981   Salesman and Cashier

Summers   J and L Hot Dogs, Belmar, NJ

1983   Partner/Operator
1982   Owned and operated hot dog wagon in resort community.
                 Net Profits--over $5,000 for two summers--used for college
                 education.

Summers   Byrne Brothers Inc., New York, NY

1980   Junior Salesman
                 Participated in all aspects of selling plumbing supplies.

1979   Sales Trainee

Interests   Skiing, tennis, and photography

References and writing samples available upon request.

Anthony Canelli:
Many Talents, Many Experiences

Special Features
- A multipurpose functional résumé
- Highlights a multitalented job seeker's various skills

The Problem. Anthony Canelli, who majored in diplomacy and world affairs, can do so many things well that he is unsure what he would like to do after graduation. His academic experiences have not been limited to his major field of study. He has minored in mathematics, performing better in his math courses than in those of his major field, and has taken course work in economics, statistics, computer sciences, and Spanish. Anthony's work experiences and extracurricular activities have also contributed to the development of his many talents and capabilities. His problem is his lack of direction.

He has been talking with a career counselor at his college's career planning and placement office in order to decide what he wants to do, but he wanted to develop a résumé he could use in the meantime—one that would be suitable for giving to on-campus interviewers and responding to posted opportunities.

The Solution. Anthony decided to stress his skills and he developed what could be called a traditional functional résumé by organizing his accomplishments under skills headings. Reviewing his accomplishments, he identified three basic skill areas that he used to create major headings. These skill areas are presented after Anthony's summary of his educational background.

Anthony felt that his liberal arts education gave him the chance to explore many different interests and that it taught him how to view problems in many different ways. Through his course work in mathematics and computer science and several employment experiences, Anthony has learned a great deal about computers and programming applications; he has therefore grouped relevant experiences under a computer skills heading. Various jobs have provided Anthony with significant experience in sales, marketing research, and management, and since these three activities are often com-bined in a single job description, Anthony decided to summarize his experience in a separate section on his résumé. And finally, because Anthony had demonstrated his responsiveness to community and social concerns by serving in political campaigns, community and college events, and the student government, he decided to highlight some of the experiences under yet another skills heading.

Format and Layout. The résumé boldly highlights each of Anthony's four headings. Typed periods effectively set off specific accomplishments associated with each heading.

Summary. The format of this résumé is that of a traditional functional résumé. Anthony directs the attention of potential employers to major skills categories rather than to specific employers and then documents his accomplishments in each category. Anthony is a person with numerous experiences, many skills, and a great deal to offer an employer. Until he can focus on specific goals, this résumé will serve very nicely. It communicates to employers that Anthony is a multitalented individual who has many abilities and not just a bright student who knows a lot about diplomacy and world affairs.

Typewritten using a Letter Gothic element. ➡

ANTHONY CANELLI

School Address: Home Address:
534 Dogwood Pl.   12 South Austin Blvd.
Apartment 23A   Champaign, IL 60644
Los Angeles, CA 90042   (312) 487-3857
(213) 259-5682

BROAD LIBERAL ARTS EDUCATION:

   OCCIDENTAL COLLEGE, Los Angeles, CA
   . Bachelor of Arts, expected June 1985
   . Major in Diplomacy and World Affairs--Major GPA 3.2/4.0
   . Minor in Mathematics--Minor GPA 3.5/4.0
   . Course work in economics, statistics, computer science, and Spanish

   AMERICAN UNIVERSITY, Washington, DC
   . Through an Occidental College program, worked for Research Council of Washington
     and completed courses in foreign affairs and government, Fall 1984.

KNOWLEDGEABLE OF COMPUTERS AND PROGRAMMING APPLICATIONS:

   . Can program in BASIC7 and PL/1 languages--GPA in computer science courses 3.45/4.0.
   . Used variety of hardware, including microcomputers.
   . As Research Associate for Research Council of Washington completed extensive
     preliminary research for marketing study of home computer sales in Europe, including
     research of various manufacturers and comparison of their products; used word
     processor to write and edit final report.
   . Developed computer database to present voting records and comparative analyses of
     voting records of California congressmen and senators on various legislative issues
     for the League of Women Voters. Summer 1984.
   . Provided statistical consulting services and developed software for study of sports
     injuries for the Occidental College Department of Physical Education. Spring 1983.

EXPERIENCED IN SALES, MARKETING RESEARCH, AND MANAGEMENT:

   . Salesperson for College Sporting Goods, Los Angeles, CA, part-time 1983--1985 while
     attending classes.
   . As Assistant Manager for College Sporting Goods, supervised full-time and part-time
     workers; developed work schedules; opened and closed store; tabulated daily
     receipts; and received shipments and maintained inventory using a computerized
     system. Summer 1982.
   . Research Council of Washington is a marketing research firm that conducts research
     on various topics. As Research Associate, undertook thorough literature searches in
     the Library of Congress; interviewed government officials and trade and industry
     experts on the telephone to develop detailed reports; and served as a research team
     leader for a project dealing with home computer sales in Europe.
   . Assistant Manager and counterworker for McDonald's, Champaign, IL. Summers and
     part-time 1980--1982.

RESPONSIVE TO COMMUNITY AND SOCIAL CONCERNS:

   . Campaigned for numerous local and national political candidates in California and
     Illinois.
   . Instructor and coach for Southern California Special Olympics. 1983--1985.
   . Elected member of Associated Students of Occidental College, student self-governing
     body, 1984--1985.

Rebecca B. Churchill:
A Music Major's Résumé Hits the High Notes

> **Special Features**
> - Targeted, combination functional and chronological résumé
> - Résumé highlights related experiences, tones down education

The Problem. A music history and literature major who did not want to teach, Rebecca Churchill decided to seek a position in personnel management. If possible, she wanted the position to involve training employees. She had much to offer a potential employer, but she needed a way to stress her qualifications.

The Solution. Rebecca felt that her greatest assets were her fund-raising and administrative experiences, and she developed a résumé that emphasized these points. The Qualifications section effectively summarizes her skills and accomplishments and supports her stated objective by highlighting her experience training personnel and developing training programs. The Related Experience section then provides the nuts-and-bolts details: her job titles, the location of her employers, and when she worked.

Rebecca does not describe her academic experiences in detail, since they are not relevant to her job-search goal. In fact, her education credits appear at the very end of the résumé.

Format and Layout. Rebecca's résumé is designed to draw attention to her greatest strengths: her focused objective and her relevant qualifications. She begins the résumé with a standard block format, in which each sentence begins at the left-hand margin and continues to the right-hand margin. After the first two headings, she uses a two-column format, which helps to emphasize the Professional Objective and Qualifications sections.

Summary. Rebecca is more than a musician; she is a person who has held positions of responsibility in both academic and work settings. By downplaying her education and describing in detail her qualifications in the areas of fund-raising, program supervision, and management, she can be confident that she is presenting herself as a person who has something to offer. Her confidence, and the résumé's documentation of her achievements, will serve her well in her job search.

Typewritten using a Prestige Elite element. ➡

REBECCA B. CHURCHILL

Box 23   7765 Wills Circle
Hollins College   Houston, Texas 77024
Roanoke, Virginia 24020   713-467-9254
703-369-9645

PROFESSIONAL OBJECTIVE

Position in personnel management. Special interest in developing and implementing personnel training programs.

QUALIFICATIONS

Developed fund-raising campaign that raised over $150,000 for Ronald McDonald House. Trained 10 team leaders and coordinated efforts of 200 volunteers. Created all training literature. Appeared on television to promote efforts. Personally responsible for corporate fund-raising.

Supervised all arts and crafts activities for YMCA day camp for three summers. Trained counselors and instructed campers in daily projects.

Retail experience with Target Stores involved training new cashiers, assisting with hiring process, and exposure to marketing and customer service.

As temporary office worker, became familiar with personnel procedures of numerous organizations.

RELATED EXPERIENCE

Ronald McDonald House   Developed campaign to raise funds to
Roanoke, Virginia   purchase and renovate house for use
Chairperson, Fund-Raising Committee by children receiving treatment for
                                     severe illnesses and their families.
                                     Part-time, 1983--85

Norrell Services, Inc.   Performed clerical and reception
Houston, Texas   duties for various organizations.
Temporary Office Worker   Summer 1984

Target Stores, Inc.   As Pharmacy Clerk, maintained
Houston, Texas   prescription files, assisted customers,
Pharmacy Clerk   and tabulated receipts. Winter 1984
Assistant Head Cashier and Cashier
                                     As Assistant Head Cashier, developed
                                     work schedules for all cashiers, took
                                     register totals, and balanced all cash
                                     drawers. Part-time 1980--82

Summer of Fun Day Camp   Planned and taught all arts and crafts
Houston, Texas   activities, budgeted for and purchased
Arts and Crafts Director   all materials, and trained counselors.
                                     Summers 1981--83

EDUCATION

Hollins College, Roanoke, Virginia   Overall Grade Point Average: 3.2/4.0
Bachelor of Arts, December 1985   Major Grade Point Average: 3.3/4.0
Major: Music History and Literature
Activities: Mu Phi Epsilon Music Fraternity
   and Student Judiciary Committee

Christopher Crockett:
Looking For a Trial Career or
"Pre-Law Preparation"

Special Features
- Boldly highlights skills before anything else
- Multipurpose résumé combining functional and chronological approaches

---

The Problem. Christopher Crockett is majoring in history and Spanish, and he thinks that he will someday attend law school, it being something of a family tradition. He is still not sure, however, that attending law school would be a conscious choice and not just an unconscious following of others' expectations. "Law school would be the easy way to go, but I would like to try something else first to give myself time to decide whether I really want to be a lawyer." Because he lacked a clear career goal, Chris created a résumé that highlights the skills he developed throughout his numerous extracurricular and work experiences.

The Solution. Chris's greatest assets are stressed at the very beginning of his résumé. Under the headings Program Design and Implementation and Research and Report Writing, he describes in active and functional terms the experiences he has had that have developed these capabilities. Under Experience Chris gives further details about these experiences: names of organizations and people he worked with, dates, locations, and so on. A potential employer who reads the entire résumé will conclude that Christopher Crockett is a person who has done a great deal in the past, and that he will continue to do a great deal in the future.

Without definite focus, but aware of at least three possible job-search directions, including international banking, translation or other work for international organizations, and a staff position in Washington, D.C., Chris created a résumé that would be appropriate for any of these (and for many other possibilities). Chris is aware that his résumé cannot be all things to all potential employers, and that he will have to stress different aspects of his past in covering letters and during interviews, depending on the requirements of the job. For positions in banking, for example, he will emphasize his research and writing skills and his ability to promote ideas. For positions that might require him to travel or deal with international organizations, he will draw attention to his foreign travel experiences and fluency in Spanish. For posts in Washington, Chris will stress his previous experiences as a congressional intern, as well as his committee work and experiences as a program planner.

Format and Layout. The layout of Chris's résumé is unique in that the listing of skills appears at the beginning of the résumé without a major introductory heading such as Skills or Summary of Skills. This is because Chris wanted to draw the attention of individual employers to specific skills, not to a total summary of his skills. As discussed, he will "target" his covering letters and interview presentations, focusing on the skills he feels would be important to a given employer. Boldface type and the use of several different type sizes and styles enable Chris to highlight words and phrases that are of most importance.

Summary. Christopher Crockett is a liberal arts graduate with a history of success. Given the opportunity he will translate past accomplishments into future successes. This résumé will help him translate his past in terms that a potential employer will understand, and that should translate into job-search success.

CHRISTOPHER CROCKETT
326 Main Street, 3E
Hanover, NH 03755   **(603) 643-2369**

PROGRAM DESIGN AND IMPLEMENTATION

Member of committee that organized and presented a three-day conference called "Nuclear Arms: Challenge and Choices." Speakers included General Alexander M. Haig, Senator Paul Tsongas, Representative Edward Markey, and Father Robert Drinan. As member of committee, assisted in developing program focus, inviting speakers, arranging transportation and accommodations for speakers, reserving facilities for seminars and speakers, and coordinating efforts of over 100 student and staff volunteers.

As **Apprentice Teacher,** developed and implemented daily lesson plans designed to fit into a total framework of course objectives.

As **Alumni Language Program Assistant,** taught, developed, and implemented lesson plans and assisted in organizing ten-day program involving participants of all ages, backgrounds, and language proficiencies. Coordinated registration and housing, organized programs, and acted as a liaison between program organizers and participants.

While serving in **numerous elected positions,** planned programs, delegated responsibilities, and oversaw work of peers to ensure program completion.

RESEARCH AND REPORT WRITING

As **Congressional Intern,** researched and analyzed policy issues and prospective legislation and wrote policy analyses and synopses. Corresponded with constituents concerning various local and national issues. Utilized Library of Congress for research.

As **Paralegal,** researched issues dealing with pending cases, searched titles, and wrote preliminary briefs.

As **Senior and Junior Class President,** wrote numerous reports to administration presenting student viewpoint on college issues.

EDUCATION

DARTMOUTH COLLEGE, Hanover, NH. Class of 1985.
Dual major in History and Spanish, concentration in history of Latin America and international affairs. Fluent in Spanish.
UNIVERSIDAD DE GRANADA, Granada, Spain.
Studied history, literature, and art as a part of Dartmouth's Language Study Abroad Program. Spring 1983.
SAN ANTONIO HIGH SCHOOL, San Antonio, TX. Class of 1981.
Delivered valedictorian address. Member of National Honor Society. President of Junior Class. President of Spanish Club.

EXPERIENCE

DARTMOUTH COLLEGE SPANISH DEPARTMENT, Hanover, NH. Winter 1984–Spring 1985.
Apprentice Teacher: Taught Spanish using Rassias method utilizing intensive language drills. Devised and presented daily drill sessions to classes of 10 to 15 students. Assisted in preparation of examinations and reviewed homework.
DARTMOUTH COLLEGE SENIOR SYMPOSIUM COMMITTEE, Hanover, NH. Winter 1984–Spring 1985.
Executive Committee Member: Involved in organization and coordination of three-day symposium that brought several nationally known speakers to campus to discuss issues related to nuclear arms development. Symposium received network news coverage.
DARTMOUTH COLLEGE ALUMNI LANGUAGE PROGRAM, Hanover, NH. Summer 1984.
Student Assistant: Working under Professor John Rassias, taught Spanish to participants of all ages. Developed and presented lessons and drill sessions. Organized logistics of ten-day program, including housing, registration, and activities. Interacted with persons of various backgrounds and taught all levels of language skills.
CROCKETT AND TAGLE, ATTORNEYS-AT-LAW, San Antonio, TX. Summers 1983 and 1982.
Paralegal: Researched issues for pending cases, searched titles, and wrote preliminary briefs. Gained working knowledge of basic legal tenets.
HONORABLE HENRY B. GONZALEZ, Washington, DC. Fall 1982.
Congressional Intern: Researched and analyzed policy issues including economic development, U.S.–Mexican relations, tax law changes, and the federal budget. Drafted responses to constituents' questions and corresponded with constituents. Served as assistant to congressman's press aide.

DARTMOUTH ACTIVITIES

Elected Senior and Junior Class President.
Member, Alpha Theta Fraternity.
Member, Paleopitus, a leadership organization that presents student viewpoints on various issues to the administration.
Member, Honorary Degree Committee.
Member, Green Key, junior honorary society that provides a wide range of services to the college community.

REFERENCES AVAILABLE UPON REQUEST.

Parker C. Davidson:
The Astronomy Major Who Wishes to Be a Star—But Where?

Special Feature
- Multipurpose chronological résumé that can be used in applying for jobs and filling out graduate school applications

---

The Problem. Like many liberal arts students, Parker C. Davidson, an astronomy major, faces a difficult decision upon graduation. He is not sure whether to seek entry-level employment or enter law school or an M.B.A. program. He seems to be a natural at sales and marketing, but he has doubts about whether, with a major in astronomy, he has adequate preparation to advance in business. He is a very ambitious person who wishes to excel at whatever he does.

In addition to considering entry-level positions in marketing and sales, as well as law-related areas, Parker wants to explore the possibility of teaching and coaching in a private secondary school for a few years prior to entering graduate school. Talented in academics, sports, and singing, he wants what he calls "a last opportunity to be in an environment where I can do all three and get paid for it."

The Solution. Parker developed a traditional chronological résumé that will enable him to present himself as a multitalented, success-oriented person. Because of its simplicity—it has only two major headings, Education and Employment—it allows Parker to direct attention to specific academic, extracurricular, or job-related items, according to his purposes. Parker's high school scholastic and athletic achievements are worth mentioning, even though they are normally omitted from a résumé. The diversity of his academic and extracurricular activities will be very attractive to private schools. He can teach science, computer science, foreign languages, and economics, as well as coach football or track and direct vocal groups.

Parker can use his résumé not only to apply for jobs but also to apply to graduate and professional schools. It will make completing applications to law schools and graduate business schools easier, for all of the background information requested on such forms appears on the résumé and will be easy for him to transcribe.

Format and Layout. Although Parker uses a traditional chronological approach, his résumé does not look boring. He uses bullets (typed periods) to highlight extracurricular and employment accomplishments. A timeline down the margin indicates when he was involved in each of his numerous activities. Parker also uses capitalization and underlining to emphasize important information.

Summary. Parker Davidson the astronomy major wants to be a star wherever he goes after graduation. The confusion he faces now will not lessen his chances of shining within any of the numerous settings he is considering. He has a résumé that is effective, and he will act assertively in communicating with persons in each of these settings.

Typewritten using a Letter Gothic element. ➡

PARKER C. DAVIDSON

School Address
3529 Montgomery Avenue
Haverford, PA 19041
(215) 648-8786

Home Address
29 Lake Forest Lane
Lake Forest, IL 62541
(312) 767-8982

EDUCATION

1981-1985   HAVERFORD COLLEGE, Haverford, PA
B.A. in Astronomy, June 1985. Overall GPA: 3.2/4.0. Academic
Honors junior year, anticipated for senior year. Course work in
macroeconomics, microeconomics, international affairs, comparative
political systems. Knowledge of BASIC and related computer
languages. Fluent in German. Proficient in French.

- Varsity Football 1982-1984--Letterman 1983 and 1984.
- Haverford A Cappella Singers 1981-1985--Musical Director
  1984-1985: arranged music for performances, conducted
  rehearsals, coordinated record album production efforts.
- Haverford Chamber Singers 1982
- Thanksgiving Food Drive and other community service projects.

1978-1981   LAKE FOREST HIGH SCHOOL, Lake Forest, IL
Graduated 16th out of class of 435, June 1981. National Honor Society.
Cum Laude Society. National Merit Commendation. Illinois State Scholar.

- Varsity Football 1978-1980--Letterman 1978, 1979, and 1980.
- Varsity Track 1979-1981--Letterman 1980 and 1981.
- Forester Singers and Madrigal and Swing vocal groups.
- Eagle Scout

EMPLOYMENT

1984-1985   NATIONAL DIRECTORY OF SUMMER INTERNSHIPS, Haverford, PA
Marketing Director
- Coordinated marketing efforts for student-published directory.
- Developed mailing list and brochures.
- Received orders and shipped directories.
- Maintained financial records.
- Efforts resulted in largest sales of directory ever--over 4000
  copies--and largest net profit--over $7,500.

1983
Summer   AMERICAN HOSPITAL SUPPLY CORPORATION, McGaw Park, IL
Market Research Intern, American Critical Care Division
- Coordinated distribution and data analysis for New Products
  Questionnaire.
- Designed and completed Sales Tracking Studies and Market Overview
  Studies.
- Assisted salespersons in direct-sales efforts.

1982 and
1981
Summers   SMITHS' MEN'S STORE, Lake Forest, IL
Salesperson
- Assisted customers with purchases.
- Tabulated sales receipts.
- Displayed merchandise and maintained stock.
- Opened and closed store.
- Trained new personnel.

PERSONAL

Interests and hobbies include politics, tennis, golf, literature, theater,
and music.

James Dawson:
A Journalist Shows His Skills and His Works

Special Features
- Combination résumé and portfolio
- Creative graphic presentation and format
- Targeted résumé including Objective statement and Qualifications section

The Problem. James Dawson's greatest assets are his job-search focus and job-related experience. This philosophy major's résumé is targeted to project a sense of direction and determination; it contains a Related Experience as well as a Qualifications section to reinforce the fact that James has had exposure to communications-industry settings and tasks. James's diverse job-related experiences are first cited in the Qualifications section and then documented in the list of employers and job titles appearing under Related Experience.

Format and Layout. Over the course of the years, while working at a number of interesting jobs in communications, James had been able to collect a number of impressive samples that could be used to demonstrate the quality of his work to potential employers. In trying to think of creative ways to present these samples, James came up with a novel idea. He made his résumé into a portfolio. (Creativity is of course one of James's strengths, and his original approach to résumé writing demonstrates this very well.)

James's résumé was printed on 17-x-11-inch paper, folded like a book. The résumé itself appears on the outside cover and his samples appear on the inside right-hand page under the heading "Samples of Work by James Dawson" (see illustration at right). Under this heading James can attach copies of his best works. He always included photos and often sent along a few writing samples as well. He based his selection of samples on the type of organization he was contacting. Thus he attached more newspaper stories when contacting newspapers and more magazine stories when contacting magazines. The finished product looks very professional and projects creativity and knowledge of layout and design.

Special Uses. James used the résumé (minus the Stanford Publishing Course entry) when applying for admission to a summer publishing course. After completing the program the summer after graduation James entered this experience under the Education heading.

Summary. By means of this special résumé James is able to tell employers about his qualifications and actually show them samples of work. James's résumé truly "shows and tells" employers that he has the skills to succeed.

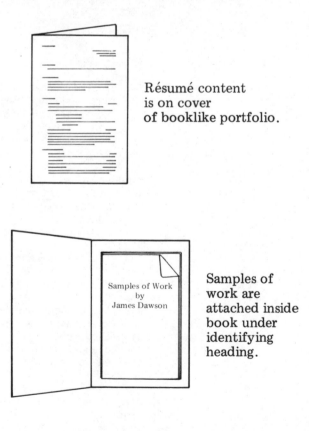

Résumé content is on cover of booklike portfolio.

Samples of Work by James Dawson

Samples of work are attached inside book under identifying heading.

JAMES DAWSON

Box 835 Trinity College
Hartford, CT 06106
(203) 527-8643

OBJECTIVE

A position requiring skills in writing, editing, and photography.

QUALIFICATIONS

Experience in magazine, newspaper, and book publishing...edited for style
and content...researched for accuracy...assigned, supplemented, and revised
stories...coordinated photographs and artwork...possess thorough command of
grammar...knowledgeable of layout and design.

EDUCATION

TRINITY COLLEGE   Hartford, CT
Bachelor of Arts degree, with major in Philosophy.
June 1985. Studied at the Institute for European Studies, London, England.

   Varsity Squash (1981-1985)
   Black Students Association (1981-1985)
   Trinity Tripod: reporter and photographer for weekly campus newspaper
      (1982-1985)

STANFORD PUBLISHING COURSE   Stanford, CA
Completed course requirements, summer 1985. Participated in seminars
presented by representatives of national publishing houses and magazines on
editorial, design, and marketing aspects of publishing. As final project,
devised editorial content, cover and interior design, and direct-mail
package for hypothetical magazine.

RELATED EXPERIENCE

WEST HARTFORD NEWS   West Hartford, CT
Reporter. Covered town news and features for weekly newspaper. (Part-time,
1983-1985)

D MAGAZINE   Dallas, TX
Intern. Edited copy, wrote articles, conducted telephone interviews and
polls, and organized photograph files. (Summer 1984)

TEXAS HOMES MAGAZINE   Dallas, TX
Intern. Edited copy, participated in house shoots, wrote letters to writers
concerning unsolicited manuscripts and story ideas, corresponded with
writers concerning assignments, and searched for article illustrations.
(Summer 1984)

DC PUBLIC RELATIONS   Dallas, TX
Account Assistant. Assisted in preparation of campaign proposals,
researched client background information, created slogans, took photographs,
and solicited new accounts. (Summer 1983)

NEW LONDON PRESS
Editorial Assistant. Proofread and pasted up copy, wrote biographies of
authors for publicity materials, and researched bibliographies. (Summer 1982)

Jennifer Drew:
From Elementary to Higher Education—
Bridging the Gap

Special Features
- Targeted functional résumé used to make the transition from one field to another
- Tranferable Skills section highlights the skills from the field of elementary education that are applicable to higher education

---

The Problem. Jennifer Drew has an undergraduate degree in elementary education and a graduate degree in bilingual education. After teaching in an elementary school bilingual education program for over four years, she now wants "out." She wants to leave the setting she is in, but she does not want to leave the field of education. She feels she would rather apply the skills she has to positions in higher education. As a result of consulting with some of her undergraduate college's alumni and going on a number of informational interviews, Jennifer became very interested in development and admissions work. Since she now had new career goals in mind, Jennifer wanted to be careful not to project the image of an elementary school teacher who was tired of "minding the kids." She wanted to present herself as a person who has direction and who has talents that are applicable to her new goals. Jennifer therefore developed a functional résumé that stressed skills, rather than job titles, degrees, or dates.

The Solution. At the head of her résumé Jennifer stresses direction and skills by using Career Goal and Transferable Skills headings. She highlights her communications, organization and program planning, and language capabilities. A potential employer reading Jennifer's résumé will perceive her as a person who has real, transferable qualifications and not just as a teacher who wants to change careers. Within the discussions of skills, Jennifer presents evidence of the abilities she gained from experiences outside of the area of elementary education. Jennifer has done much more than just teach young people; she has organized events, planned programs, raised funds, and been involved in numerous activities that required various skills and capabilities. By writing a targeted covering letter, Jennifer can describe in more detail the skills and experiences that would be applicable to a particular employer. She can elaborate upon her fund-raising activities when applying for development jobs and highlight her communications, sales, and evaluation skills when applying for admissions positions.

Format and Layout. Jennifer developed a résumé that presents her as a person who is capable of functioning well within higher education. By presenting skills at the beginning of the résumé—following a statement of career goal—and her teaching positions and academic training in elementary education at the end, Jennifer succeeds in doing what all career changers must do—she builds a "skills bridge" from the past to the future. Jennifer's résumé tells potential employers that what she has done can be applied to what she will do in future jobs.

Summary. Jennifer is not just a collection of job titles and academic degrees. She is a person who is capable of performing the tasks associated with her new job-search targets, and her résumé shows a potential employer that this is the case. It bridges the gap between elementary education and student services positions in higher education.

Typewritten using a Prestige Elite element. ➡

JENNIFER DREW

229 Brokenbend Road   213-746-3953
Los Angeles, CA 90017

CAREER GOAL

To utilize the following skills in a position in higher education. Special
interest in development and admissions.

TRANSFERABLE SKILLS

Communications
Chaired fund-raising events for school and church groups.

Retail sales experience.

Communicated weekly with parents regarding students' progress and with school
administrators concerning all classroom activities.

Counseled students on personal issues and academic concerns.

Trained and supervised student teachers.

Worked with patients and staff in the emergency room of UCLA Medical Center on a
volunteer basis.

Organization and Program Planning
Motivated and organized classes of approximately 25 students in group and
individual activities in two languages.

Developed individualized programs to help students attain specific objectives.

Assisted in creating and implementing a local School Improvement Plan that
increased efficiency of programs and improved community relations.

Consistently and accurately completed detailed federal, state, and local
documentation on time.

Languages
Fluent in Spanish. Familiar with French.

EDUCATION

M.Ed. University of California, Los Angeles, Westwood, CA.
       Bilingual Education, December 1983. Course work in Education Administration.

B.A.   Hiram College, Hiram, OH.
       Elementary Education, June 1980.

EMPLOYMENT HISTORY

Los Angeles Unified School District, Bilingual Teacher, 1981-present.
Cleveland Independent School District, Student Teacher, 1979--1980.
Davidson's Department Store, Cleveland, OH, Salesperson, part-time and summers
1976-1979.

ACTIVITIES AND ASSOCIATIONS

Hiram College Alumni Association, Class of 1980 Vice President.
UCLA Medical Center, Volunteer.
American Association of Bilingual Educators.
American Teachers Association.

Kathy Fish:
Presenting Career-Transferable Skills

Special Features
- Multipurpose résumé suitable for more than one job-search interest
- Career-Transferable Skills section

The Problem. Kathy Fish, who majored in government, suffered from the so-called "plight of the liberal arts graduate." She believed that her education had given her nothing to present to a potential employer and that she had no "marketable skills." A visit to her college's career planning and placement office "cured" Kathy, or perhaps "rediagnosed" her ailment. Kathy suffered from "lack of awareness and lack of confidence"—she was unaware of all of the skills she possessed and had no confidence in her ability to present herself to a potential employer as a person worth hiring. Although she had not defined specific goals, Kathy did have a résumé that she was proud of and some idea of where she was looking.

The Solution. Self-assessment and the completion of a skills flowchart made Kathy aware of the many qualities she had to offer an employer. Research into career options gave her some ideas about which areas to focus on. As of the time she wrote her résumé, the fields she had tentatively settled on included banking operations, state government, and college student personnel. Kathy felt that banking operations would be an excellent setting in which to utilize almost all of her skills and her course work in economics, accounting, and computer programming. Her interest in state government stems from her experiences with a political campaign, and her interest in college student personnel stems from her work in the financial aid office of her college. The résumé Kathy developed can be used effectively in each of these areas.

Kathy's assessment of her skills enabled her to create the section that appears at the bottom of her résumé, appropriately titled "Career-Transferable Skills." Under each type of skill, she outlines the experience she has had that most directly involved use of the skill. In her communications with potential employers, in cover letters and during interviews, Kathy will draw upon this portion of her résumé to support her candidacy for employment.

If Kathy becomes more interested in one of the above three areas than the others, she can target her résumé by adding a statement of objective and by reworking the skills section. If she decides on banking operations, for example, she can change the heading to "Banking Skills," use the same skill headings, and add to the descriptions analyses of how they would enhance her performance as a person working within bank operations. For now, she is pleased with the résumé as it is.

Format and Layout. Kathy's résumé is fairly conservative in appearance, which is appropriate for the fields she is considering entering. She used capitalization to create prominent headings and underlining to make some of the most important phrases stand out. One of the best features of this résumé is the Career-Transferable Skills section. Kathy chose to save the best for last, summarizing her qualifications and the skills she acquired from all of the experiences cited under the Education and Experience headings as well as from some experiences not cited.

Summary. This résumé presents Kathy's assets very well. For Kathy the cure for the plight of the liberal arts student was a dose of awareness and self-confidence brought about by a careful and thoughtful assessment of her skills and the resulting realization that she too could produce a very professional-looking résumé for herself.

Typewritten using a Letter Gothic element. ➡

KATHY FISH

Home Address   School Address
198 Vine Street   352B Main Street
Damariscotta, Maine   04543   Brunswick, Maine   04011
207-563-1972   207-724-3356

EDUCATION

Bowdoin College   Brunswick, ME
Bachelor of Arts, May 1985. Honors major in Government (GPA 3.4/4.0), with emphasis
on analysis and comparisons of political systems.

Courses included international organizations, macroeconomics, microeconomics,
international economics, accounting, and computer programming (BASIC and BASIC 7).

Foreign study in Paris, France. Fluent in French. College exchange with Dartmouth
College, fall 1983.

Class of 1985 Executive Committee. Inter-Dormitory Committee. Dormitory Chairperson
1982. Women's Track. Women's Rugby. Glee Club. Intramural Sports.

Lincoln Academy   Newcastle, ME
Graduated Valedictorian, June 1981. Selected for AFS International Student Exchange
to Salvador, Brazil, 1980. National Honor Society. Senior Class President. Maine
Scholar's Day Delegate.

EXPERIENCE

Bowdoin College Office of Financial Aid   Brunswick, ME
Student Assistant. Assist students in completing financial aid forms. Review
applications, calculating need analyses and submitting forms to financial aid
officers for final decisions. Complete work-study and other federal paperwork.
Maintain student files. (September 1984--present)

Bowdoin College Government Department   Brunswick, ME
Research Assistant. Aided professor with research project. Results presented at an
international symposium in Rio de Janeiro, Brazil. (March-June 1983)

The Cheechako Restaurant   Damariscotta, ME
Waitress. Supervised dining-room personnel. Analyzed and accounted for dining-room
receipts.   (Summers 1982, 1981, and 1980)

Assumed full responsibility for meeting costs of college education.

CAREER-TRANSFERABLE SKILLS

Research and Analytical Skills
Selected as research assistant by professor in Government department. Gathered and
analyzed data regarding the effect of economic factors in the formation of political
systems in Spain and Portugal. Developed and conducted independent research study
dealing with politicization of children; results were used in research paper.

Organizational Skills
Assisted with design and coordination of 300-person telephone survey concerning
campaign issues involved in Maine Senate Race, 1982. Recruited and trained
surveyors. Wrote reports concerning results. Maintained financial aid files for
over 750 students.

Interpersonal Skills
Experienced in training and managing fellow workers, counseling peers, and representing
peers in elected positions. Lived with two non-English-speaking families as part of
foreign-study experiences. Advised and counseled students on financial aid issues.
Motivated volunteer workers to contribute time and money to political campaign.

Elaine S. Fletcher:
Back to Work for Someone Who Never Stopped

Special Features
- Résumé for re-entry into the job market highlights many accomplishments
- Qualifications section summarizes greatest strengths

The Problem. Elaine S. Fletcher wants to re-enter the working world after ten years spent caring for her family, and she needs to let potential employers in on all the things she accomplished while she wasn't "working." Although she wasn't paid for her labors, Elaine was a very active member of her community. She held positions of responsibility on various committees, positions that allowed her to develop and utilize skills that are applicable to conventional work settings. Elaine had also continued to pursue her educational interests. In order to show employers that she hadn't only been keeping house and raising a family, Elaine developed a résumé that presents her as someone who never stopped learning and participating.

The Solution. Elaine is what one would call a "doer"; she is always actively involved in something. After graduation from college, Elaine started working for an insurance company. With the birth of her first child Elaine stopped working for the insurance company, but she didn't stop doing. She began taking adult-education classes at a local high school and, not being one to just take classes, she became very actively involved in the administration of the adult-education program. Because of her work experiences with the insurance company and with the savings and loan, and because she had taken accounting, Elaine was eventually elected to be an Executive Board Member. In that capacity, she became involved in the board of education's Administrative Review Committee. As if that weren't enough, Elaine was also an active member of her church's College and Services Outreach Program (a program she herself developed several years ago) and a leader of a Brownie Girl Scout troop.

It should be clear by now that Elaine never really stopped working after she left the in-surance company. She continued to grow as a person—and as a potential employee—developing and utilizing skills that should be of interest to many employers. Although Elaine is unsure of exactly what type of job she wants, she is sure that she is ready to return to the so-called "working world." The Career Decision Making course Elaine took at a local community college got her started on the career decision-making process and taught her some very useful research and job-search techniques. Elaine will use the résumé she developed as an exercise for that class in order to communicate with potential employers.

Format and Layout. Elaine had her résumé typeset in order to project a very businesslike image and to show employers that she is serious about finding a job. Her résumé starts with a Qualifications section that presents a summary of all the skills Elaine developed over the course of the years. Elaine decided to highlight her educational background, not because she wanted to put her Home Economics degree to use, but because she was proud of the fact that she has never stopped learning. She listed several of the community college and adult-education courses she had taken. Under Community Leadership Elaine details the various positions she held that involved hours and hours of work and required many different skills.

Summary. Elaine did not stop learning or working after she left her job with the insurance company over ten years ago. She will use this résumé to find another job in which she can apply all that she has learned over the years. She will no doubt continue to work as hard in a paid position as she has in her volunteer capacities.

Typeset in Univers. ➡

ELAINE S. FLETCHER

223 Burgundy Drive
Flint, Michigan 48506
(313) 762-9753

QUALIFICATIONS

Experienced bookkeeper and organizer. Capable of maintaining Accounts Receivable and Accounts Payable. Capable of supervising others and motivating others to maintain optimum performance levels. Can develop and implement projects, paying attention to detail and meeting deadlines. Have worked on committees and in group settings. Have established performance standards and evaluated employees' performance.

EDUCATION

MICHIGAN STATE UNIVERSITY, East Lansing, Michigan
Bachelor of Arts in Home Economics, June 1973.
LANSING COMMUNITY COLLEGE, Lansing, Michigan (1969–1971)

Additional Educational Experiences:

MOTT COMMUNITY COLLEGE, Flint, Michigan
"Introduction to Home Computers," Spring 1983
"Career Decision Making," Fall 1982
"Introduction to Accounting," Fall 1973

FLINT HIGH SCHOOL ADULT EDUCATION PROGRAM, Flint, Michigan
"Management Skills," Winter 1980
"Group Dynamics," Winter 1979
"Personal Financial Management," Winter 1978
"European Art," Winter 1977
"Interior Decorating," Winter 1976

EMPLOYMENT BACKGROUND

MINNESOTA MUTUAL LIFE INSURANCE CO., Flint, Michigan (1973–1975)
As Group Claims Coordinator, coordinated transactions and maintained records of all health-care and hospitalization claims. Recorded additions, deletions, conversions, payments, and reconciliations, and acted upon claim-eligibility requests. Handled mail and telephone inquiries and corresponded directly with subscribers.

LANSING SAVINGS AND LOAN, Lansing, Michigan (summers and part-time 1970–1973)
As Teller, handled all banking transactions, including checking, savings, loan and mortgage payments, and savings bonds.

COMMUNITY LEADERSHIP

FLINT HIGH SCHOOL ADULT EDUCATION PROGRAM, Flint, Michigan (1977–present)
As Treasurer, maintain all financial records and administer budget of over $50,000 each year. (1978–present)
As Executive Board Member, develop goals and policies for adult education program, interview and hire instructors, and interact with board of education members concerning budget and policy matters. (1977–present)

FLINT BOARD OF EDUCATION ADMINISTRATIVE REVIEW COMMITTEE, Flint, Michigan (1983–present)
As Committee Member, interview teachers and administrators concerning academic and administrative policies, evaluate policies and personnel, and make recommendations to the board of education. The purpose of the committee is to identify inefficiency, eliminate duplicated efforts, and cut $1,500,000 from the budget.

MAPLE AVENUE METHODIST CHURCH, Flint, Michigan (1975–present)
Wrote proposal that resulted in College and Service Outreach Program for college students and persons in the armed services who are church members. Solicited church sponsor families to communicate with program members while they were away at school or on duty. Maintain complete records of all program members. Administered program 1975–1977. Remain active in program as sponsor and as member of coordinating committee.

GIRL SCOUTS OF AMERICA—FLINT COUNCIL, Flint, Michigan (1981–present)
As Girl Scout Leader, responsible for troop of approximately 15 girls. Plan and coordinate activities and maintain troop financial records.

REFERENCES

Available upon request.

Cathy Lynne Giles:
Banking Past, Present, and Future

Special Features
- Targeted résumé with very focused statement of career goal
- Banking Qualifications section reviews credentials specific to job-search goal
- A Sales Experience heading highlights corollary experience

Cathy Lynne Giles is a very focused individual. She knows that she wants to be a lending officer in a commercial bank. Whether she enters the field through a formalized lending training program or through an entry-level position that will at least provide some exposure to lending matters very little to her. Fortunately, Cathy has had a significant amount of experience in banking. Several of her summer and part-time jobs in banks have already taught her a lot about the nature of the work and helped her decide on her career goal.

Cathy targets her résumé by using Career Goal, Banking Qualifications, Banking Experience, and Sales Experience headings. Her goal is stated at the very beginning of the résumé, and the Qualifications section, appearing immediately after the goal statement, summarizes all of the qualities that would make Cathy a good candidate. Cathy does not include the names of organizations she has worked for in the Qualifications section, but she does make clear references to the types of experiences she has had. Names, dates, and details about her jobs are presented in the following sections of Cathy's résumé. To help orient potential employers and to emphasize the fact that she has had experience both in banking and in retail and direct sales, Cathy grouped her listings of former jobs under two separate headings.

Format and Layout. This combined functional and chronological format is truly the best for someone like Cathy who has both a clear job-search target and related experiences. It will be obvious to anyone who reads the résumé that Cathy is qualified for the position she seeks.

Even though she majored in economics, Cathy felt that her work experiences would do more to help her get a job than would her education, so she listed her academic credentials after her work history. Note that Cathy included the names, addresses, and phone numbers of former employers who agreed to provide references; printing this information on the résumé can help save time during the application process.

Summary. Cathy's résumé speaks for itself. It is well written and well presented, and Cathy's goals and qualifications come across loudly and clearly. Cathy has worked in banks while in college; the résumé she has developed will ensure that she will be able to do so after graduation.

CATHY LYNNE GILES
232 Aldridge Avenue
Winter Park, Florida 32789
(305) 645-8922

CAREER GOAL

Commercial bank lending officer.

BANKING QUALIFICATIONS

Experience in banking and researching banking-related legislation. Commitment to a career in banking.

Course work in economics, including money and banking, accounting, finance, computer science, and research techniques.

Retail and direct-sales experience.

Possess the skills required to research loan applicants and assess risk of potential loans. Can sell successfully and maintain good relationships with customers.

BANKING EXPERIENCE

1984-1985 **WINTER PARK BANK AND TRUST COMPANY.** Winter Park, Florida.
Teller (15 hours/week)
Performed all teller transactions, including checking, savings, and certificates of deposit. Answered inquiries concerning bank services. Opened new accounts.

Summers **NORTHPARK NATIONAL BANK,** Dallas, Texas.
1983 and *Trust Department Intern* (full-time)
1984 Developed efficient procedure for processing stock and bond certificates of various banks to be exchanged for holding-company stock. Prepared weekly progress reports for large trust funds and created an indexing and filing system for quick retrieval of information in the forms of summaries and original reports.

Winter **STATE SENATOR MARYANN MATHERS,** Tallahassee, Florida.
1983 *Administrative Assistant* (full-time)
Briefed Senator on legislation. Researched and drafted bills. Attended committee meetings. Corresponded with constituents. Completed primary research on bill regarding interstate banking.

SALES EXPERIENCE

Summer **SANGER-HARRIS,** Dallas, Texas.
1982 *Sportswear Salesperson* (full-time)
Assisted customers with selections. Maintained inventory records and tabulated department sales on daily, weekly, and monthly bases.

1979-1982 **MARY KAY COSMETICS,** Dallas, Texas.
Sales Associate/Consultant (part-time and summers)
Assessed individual customer's needs and sold cosmetics and beauty supplies. Made numerous presentations to large gatherings. Always achieved sales goals. Was youngest person to be promoted to Consultant level.

EDUCATION

1981-1985 **ROLLINS COLLEGE,** Winter Park, Florida.
Bachelor of Arts, anticipated June 1985.
Major: Economics.
Banking-related course work: Macroeconomics, Microeconomics, Introduction to Accounting, Money and Banking, International Finance, Fundamentals of Computer Science (FORTRAN and COBOL), Analyses of Political Systems, and Research Methodologies.

REFERENCES

Mr. Ralph Stanky
Vice President
Manager, Trust Department
Northpark National Bank
P.O. Box 2319
Dallas, Texas 75294
(214) 783-7777

Ms. Linda Motek
Vice President, Operations
Winter Park Bank and Trust Company
P.O. Box 222
Winter Park, Florida 32788
(305) 643-9988

State Senator Maryann Mathers
State Capitol, 3-784
Tallahassee, Florida 32304

Gloria E. Glenn:
From Sociology to Computer Sales

Special Features
- Skills and Qualifications section used to focus attention on goal-related skills and experiences
- Résumé shows a sociology major can project herself as the ideal candidate for a computer-sales job
- Targeted résumé can be broadened for other objectives

The Problem. Gloria Glenn's major and the degree she will receive bear little direct application to her job-search goal. But Gloria does possess the background and motivation to succeed in a sales-oriented environment. She has worked in retail sales throughout high school and college and has promoted herself and her ideas while participating in numerous extracurricular activities.

The Solution. Developing a Professional Objective statement to target her résumé was easy for Gloria. A review of her past accomplishments and of her present interests led her to the conclusion that a position in computer hardware or software sales would be ideal. Having reached this conclusion, Gloria then spent a great deal of time carefully developing the Skills and Qualifications section; this is the "hook" of her résumé, the part that will catch the attention of prospective employers. It serves as a preface of sorts and is intended to motivate a potential employer to read beyond the first page. A well thought-out Skills and Qualifications section can also influence the decision-making process in a positive way.

Some of the courses and experiences Gloria had at the University of Oklahoma and Lamar University are of course directly applicable to her job-search goal, but Gloria chose to put Educational Background at the end of her résumé. She highlights factors she judges more important at the beginning, citing course work in calculus, statistics, computer science, and research techniques in the Skills and Qualifications section rather than in Educational Background.

Special Uses. If Gloria wished to develop a second résumé to use to apply for entry-level positions outside of the area of technical sales, all she would have to do is eliminate the statement of objective and the "technical knowledge" section from her listing of Skills and Qualifications.

Format and Layout. Gloria's résumé is conservative in format and design, but it is innovative in the way it documents Gloria's abilities to perform the tasks required of a successful salesperson.

Summary. Gloria's résumé does what she wants to do upon graduation. IT SELLS! Her résumé is not a passive documentation of past experiences, but an active presentation of the abilities she has to succeed. The focus of her Professional Objective and the qualities projected in the Skills and Qualifications section reveal that Gloria knows what she wants and is prepared to go out and get it. She has shown that she can analyze a situation and the needs of a potential buyer, develop a market strategy, and make an effective presentation. She has done so with her résumé!

GLORIA E. GLENN

School Address
14 Allenhurst
Norman, Oklahoma 73071
(918) 662-8877

Home Address
223 Chambless Drive
Beaumont, Texas 77705
(713) 236-8894

PROFESSIONAL OBJECTIVE

Position in computer hardware or software sales.

SKILLS AND QUALIFICATIONS

Technical knowledge: Courses in calculus, statistics, computer science, and research techniques all utilized computer software programming and hardware. Knowledgeable of FORTRAN, BASIC, and SPSS. Wrote "Computers and College," a research paper exploring increased emphasis on computer-related courses and the development of computer usage skills in higher education. Developed database and retrieval program for alumni fund-raising efforts.

Communications skills: Numerous activities required developing ideas, organizing tasks, motivating people to accomplish goals, and delegating responsibility. Course work in sociology and psychology developed analytical perspective. Can communicate well one on one and in groups. Comfortable presenting ideas to large audiences.

Sales ability: As campus leader, sold ideas and persuaded others to compromise or agree upon a common goal. As retail salesperson, developed sales-presentation skills and sales perspective. Confident of sales abilities. Profit-motivated.

EXTRACURRICULAR ACTIVITIES

GAMMA PHI BETA SORORITY, University of Oklahoma
Pledge Chairperson: Developed and implemented pledge training program for 45 pledges. (1985)
Panhellenic Delegate: As liaison between sorority and Panhellenic Council, worked with other sorority and fraternity representatives to promote and regulate the Panhellenic system. (1983-1984)

UNIVERSITY OF OKLAHOMA STUDENT FOUNDATION
Public Relations Committee: Promoted campus activities and events to students and alumni. (1983-1985)

UNIVERSITY OF OKLAHOMA ALUMNI ASSOCIATION
Computer Assistant: Developed database and retrieval system to identify alumni, note past contacts by Alumni Association, and note whether contributions were made. Used to increase effectiveness of fund-raising efforts. (1985)
Fund-raising Volunteer: Called alumni and solicited contributions during annual fund-raising drives. (1983-1985)

UNIVERSITY OF OKLAHOMA ADMISSIONS OFFICE
Tour Guide: Conducted tours for prospective students and their families. (1983-1985)

WORK EXPERIENCE

JEANS FOR US, Beaumont, Texas.
Salesperson: Assisted customers with selections, maintained inventory-control procedures, and assisted with buying and merchandise displays. (Summers 1981-1985)

JOSKE'S, Beaumont, Texas.
Salesperson: Assisted customers and operated cash register. (Part-time through high school and summer 1980)

EDUCATIONAL BACKGROUND

UNIVERSITY OF OKLAHOMA, Norman, Oklahoma.
Bachelor of Arts in Sociology, May 1985.
LAMAR UNIVERSITY, Beaumont, Texas. (1981-1982)

REFERENCES

A list of references will be provided upon request.

William S. Hanover:
An English Major's Presentation Is Worth a Thousand Words

Special Features
- Activities given most significance for they most reflect qualifications
- Targeted résumé with Objective statement that allows for options

The Problem. William Hanover, an English major, is a man of many talents. His academic pursuits trained him in written communications, his extracurricular activities throughout high school and college involved him in numerous publicity and promotional efforts, and he is an accomplished artist. After thoroughly researching potential career fields, William concluded that either magazine or book publishing was the field that offered him the most flexibility and the best opportunity to use his many capabilities. He wanted a résumé that showed all of his talents, not one that focused on one or two.

The Solution. William created a résumé that stresses the many extracurricular activities through which he developed publishing-related skills and that, by its design, illustrates his creativity. The résumé begins with an Objective that is specific yet includes several options. The remainder of the résumé describes the experiences William has had in each of the areas of publishing that appear in the Objective. William has developed writing and editing skills through his course work, his experiences as a legal assistant, and, above all, his work on numerous promotional materials. He has developed his abilities in design and illustration, as well as in promotions and advertising, through all of his extracurricular activities. These skills are the most important assets he has to offer, and his résumé demonstrates that he has been very active in developing them.

Supporting Materials. William intends to distribute a portfolio containing samples of his work along with his résumé. To personalize his portfolio, he decided to have his name and a creative yet conservative border printed on the cover. He also had the same border printed on the stationery he bought to use for covering letters. Both pieces are illustrated below. The picture that the résumé, portfolio, and stationery paint is truly worth a thousand words. A job-search presentation package as creative and informative as this one is sure to be effective.

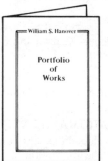

Portfolio is created by folding 17-x-11-page like a book. Copies of selected works are placed in folder and sent with résumé to potential employers. Portfolio is printed on the same kind of paper used for the résumé.

Stationery is created by printing border and heading on the same kind of paper used for the résumé.

Typewritten using a Letter Gothic element. ➡

WILLIAM S. HANOVER

OBJECTIVE: Entry-level position in publishing in any of the following areas:
. Promotions   . Advertising   . Design   . Editing

EDUCATION: **MIDDLEBURY COLLEGE**, Middlebury, VT
Will graduate June, 1985, with B.A. in English.
Dean's list, sophomore and junior years.
Strong background in studio art.
Fluent in French.
Computer programming knowledge of BASIC.

LA JOLLA HIGH SCHOOL, La Jolla, CA
Graduated June 1981 with Academic Distinction.
National Merit Letter of Commendation.

Activities included: Student Government Publicity Committee, Student Newspaper (received state recognition for my editorial cartoons), Speech and Debate, Drama Club. Designed school symbol.

MIDDLEBURY ACTIVITIES: **ADVERTISING CLUB**, President and Founding Member: Directed activities and coordinated projects of student organization established to publicize and promote services of college offices and on-campus events.

SEARCH COMMITTEE FOR DIRECTOR OF CAREER COUNSELING AND PLACEMENT, Student Chairperson: Chaired student interviewing committee and presented findings to Faculty and Administration Search Committees.

ALUMNI-IN-RESIDENCE STEERING COMMITTEE, Student Director: Participated in review and selection of alumni to participate in week-long programs dealing with topical issues ranging from careers to the nuclear freeze movement.

MIDDLEBURY WINTER CARNIVAL COMMITTEE, Member: Designed T-shirt and publicity poster and assisted in planning and execution of all phases of annual event.

1984 CLASS COMMITTEE, Member: Planned and produced publicity for several campus events sponsored by committee to raise funds for class.

SIGMA PHI EPSILON, Publicity Officer, Pledge Trainer, Assistant Rush Chairperson: Promoted fraternity functions, planned rush and pledge activities, designed flyers for fraternity events. Elected "Most Valuable Brother," junior year.

EMPLOYMENT EXPERIENCE: **WILMER, CUTLER AND PICKERING**, Washington, D.C.
Legal Assistant/Librarian: Participated in research for several cases. Performed all aspects of case administration, including writing of preliminary briefs and interviewing of potential witnesses. Provided reference assistance to other Legal Assistants and Attorneys and maintained legal library. Summer 1984

BASKIN-ROBBINS 31 FLAVORS, La Jolla, CA
Waiter and Cashier. Summers 1983, 1982, and 1981

ADDRESSES: Box 498
Middlebury College
Middlebury, VT 05753
802-388-8747

54 Hillside Drive
La Jolla, CA 92037
619-455-9828
(after June 30, 1985)

Lawrence Herder:
Many Years with Few Employers and Now Forced to Make a Change

Special Features
- Objective statement that leads into a summary of qualifications
- Targeted résumé highlights qualifications for job change

The Problem. Lawrence Herder has had over 20 years of experience. After graduating from college, he spent two years in the military, promoted conference services for a hotel chain for two years, and then filled several positions for a large retail organization for a period of nine years. For the past eight years he has been the Vice President of Sales and Marketing for an office-supplies and furniture distributor. When Lawrence left J.C. Penney to work for Offices Midwest, he was sure it would be his last job change. Lawrence was very security conscious, and he was happy to be working as a manager for a successful and growing operation like Offices Midwest. But when Offices Midwest was purchased by a larger company, Lawrence was asked to leave, even though he had held an important position within the company.

Lawrence first had to overcome some psychological and practical barriers before he could go back to job hunting. As someone who had not looked for a job in over 18 years (Offices Midwest had come looking for him), Lawrence was rusty and unsure about how to proceed. Lawrence is a confident individual who has a long history of career success, but the prospect of job hunting can make the most secure individual anxious, especially when that individual has suddenly been pulled out of what he thought was a secure job. After a great deal of thinking about why he had been successful in the jobs he had held in the past and what he wanted in the future, and after meeting several times with a career counselor, Lawrence developed some solid job-search targets and dependable strategies. Lawrence came to realize along the way that he did not really want to go back to retailing or the office-supplies business. After working through the many variables that confront career changers, Lawrence ultimately decided to look for a job in advertising sales with a television or radio station.

The Solution. Because the field of advertising sales was related to his previous jobs, Lawrence created a résumé that ties his Objective statement together with a discussion of qualifications and past experiences. The capsule summary of qualifications is joined to the statement of objective; this technique helps Lawrence to convey to potential employers the fact that he is very much aware of his job-search target and that he has the qualifications to perform the tasks associated with this job. The job descriptions appearing under the Employment heading highlight only general responsibilities because Lawrence did not want to appear to be "overqualified" and because he wanted potential employers to focus on the analysis of qualifications that appears in the statement of objective.

Format and Layout. Lawrence's résumé combines the chronological and functional approaches. It has a statement of objective that includes a summary of qualifications, and this is followed by an Employment section that presents Lawrence's work history in reverse chronological order.

Summary. Lawrence's story is that of a person who has had a successful career for many years and has been forced by circumstances to undertake a job search again after some 20 years of continuous employment. Having taken some time off to regroup and re-evaluate his skills, Lawrence established new goals and came up with a new résumé that effectively linked his qualifications to his new objective.

LAWRENCE HERDER

756 Buffalo Avenue
Chicago, Illinois 62617
(312) 263-8645

OBJECTIVE

Advertising sales position that builds on the following skills and experiences:

- *Over 20 years in sales-related capacities.*
- *Capable of making direct, person-to-person contact with agency media buyers and client advertising personnel.*
- *Knowledgeable of client perspective and retail advertising strategies. Have dealt with advertising salespersons as Vice President of Sales and Marketing and Store Manager.*
- *Comfortable making group presentations, using quantitative data to support objectives. Can develop and use statistics as part of sales campaign. Have used personal computers.*
- *Academic background in communications.*

EMPLOYMENT

1977-present
OFFICES MIDWEST, Chicago, Illinois
VICE PRESIDENT OF SALES AND MARKETING

- *Responsible for all sales and marketing activities of office-supplies and furniture distributor with four retail outlets and sales force of 25. Manage direct contact, catalog, and retail sales efforts.*
- *Hire, train, and supervise all sales representatives and retail sales personnel.*
- *Create weekly newspaper advertisements and oversee publication of annual catalog and monthly sales brochures.*

1969-1977
J.C. PENNEY CO. MIDWEST DIVISION, Chicago, Illinois
STORE MANAGER–Evanston Mall Store (1973-1977)

- *Complete responsibilities for store operations.*

BUYER–Photographic Equipment and Office Supplies (1971-1973)

- *Buying and pricing responsibilities for 20 stores.*

MANAGEMENT TRAINEE (1969-1971)

- *Completed rotational program involving Department Manager, Assistant Buyer, and Assistant Store Manager positions.*

1965-1966
GREAT WESTERN HOTELS, Seattle, Washington
SALES REPRESENTATIVE/CONFERENCE COORDINATOR

- *Traveled throughout Midwest soliciting conference business for hotels in Great Western group.*
- *Made individual and group presentations, wrote contracts, and acted as liaison between client and hotels.*

EDUCATION

NORTHWESTERN UNIVERSITY, Evanston, Illinois
BACHELOR OF ARTS IN COMMUNICATIONS, 1963

PERSONAL DATA

Married   2 Children   Willing to travel
Military Service: United States Army 1963-1965

Robert D. Jay:
Is Retail Really Right, Robert?

Special Features
- Targeted résumé with statement of objective
- Effective use of skills headings highlights diverse background

---

The Problem. With a major in psychology and a minor in computer science, Robert D. Jay had a varied academic background. He also had a wide range of extracurricular and employment experiences to his credit. By the time he graduated from college, he had worked in a bank, been an accounting tutor, represented a T-shirt printing company, and held almost every position possible with a college radio station.

When it came time for Robert to decide upon his postgraduation employment goals, he had some difficulty. After doing a great deal of research—reading articles and books and interviewing alumni about their careers—Robert decided that retail management offered the diversity he sought in a career field. But, like many liberal arts job seekers, Robert did not want to "limit his possibilities," so, in addition to duplicating the targeted résumé shown here, he produced an alternate—multipurpose—version by taking off the lead-in Objective statement.

The Solution. Because Robert had done so many different things, he decided it was important to present himself in as organized a fashion as possible. He created a fairly conservative résumé, but used skill headings to highlight his varied experiences.

A retailer reviewing this résumé would probably regard Robert as a qualified candidate. Robert has had sales experience and is accomplished in the areas of finance, accounting, and basic management. And, beyond that, Robert has stated that he has a strong interest in retailing. The three Experience categories and the Computer Languages and Skills section all present information that would be of interest to employers in retailing and in numerous other industries as well.

Format and Layout. Robert's résumé is intentionally conservative in its approach and presentation. It is typed and shows the use of capitalization for headings and underlining for job titles. The Computer Languages and Skills heading was placed at the bottom because of the growing importance of these skills in all fields. Robert included this heading in the hope that it would attract the attention of employers from several different industries.

ROBERT D. JAY

University of Connecticut   269 Turkey Trot Lane
P.O. Box 367   Woodbridge, CT 06478
Storrs, CT 06268   (203) 794-3832
(203) 485-9868

OBJECTIVE
Position in a retail management-training program.

EDUCATION
UNIVERSITY OF CONNECTICUT, Storrs, CT.
Candidate for B.A. degree, June 1985. Major in psychology. Minor in computer science.
Course work in economics and accounting. Member of Kappa Kappa Kappa fraternity.

AMITY REGIONAL SENIOR HIGH SCHOOL, Woodbridge, CT.
Diploma received, June 1981. Scholastic honors for junior and senior years.

SALES AND PROMOTION EXPERIENCE
EXPRESS YOURSELF, Storrs, CT.
Campus Representative, fall 1984--spring 1985.
Planned campus advertisements for professional silkscreening company that specializes in
T-shirts and caps. Placed and delivered orders. Commission sales.

WUCR, Storrs, CT.
Promotions Director, spring 1983.
Coordinated all promotional efforts of college radio station, including two large
concert promotions and a fund-raising drive for the station.

UNIVERSITY OF CONNECTICUT OFFICE OF ADMISSIONS, Storrs, CT.
Tour Guide, spring 1983--spring 1985.
Conducted informational tours for prospective students and families. Attended two Amity
Regional Senior High School College Nights as University of Connecticut representative.

MANAGEMENT AND OFFICE EXPERIENCE
UNIVERSITY OF CONNECTICUT CAREER CENTER, Storrs, CT.
Student Assistant, fall 1984.
Maintained complete listings of temporary and permanent jobs on computer database.
Implemented data-manipulation software. Assisted in developing software to coordinate
on-campus recruiting sign-up procedure. Counseled students seeking employment.

WUCR, Storrs, CT.
Served as Programming Director, Chief Announcer, Training Director, and Promotions
Director for college radio station, spring 1982--spring 1985.

ACCOUNTING AND FINANCE EXPERIENCE
UNIVERSITY OF CONNECTICUT DEPARTMENT OF ACCOUNTING, Storrs, CT.
Tutor, spring and summer 1984.
Tutored and graded students in Introduction to Accounting. Responsibilities involved
daily interaction with small groups and individual students.

UNION TRUST COMPANY TAX DEPARTMENT, New Haven, CT.
Tax Intern, spring 1983 and spring 1984.
Assembled and proofread tax summaries and forms. Ensured that filing and payment
deadlines were met. Worked independently.

COMPUTER LANGUAGES AND SKILLS
Fluent in BASIC and PL/1. Knowledge of FORTRAN and Pascal. Experience with
microcomputers and minicomputers as well as mainframe units.

Raymond Krieger:
An Art Major Who Does Not Want to Be Painted into a Corner

> **Special Feature**
> - Highlights experience, downplays art background

The Problem. Raymond Krieger majored in studio art but, after a very thorough and difficult self-assessment, he concluded that he did not have enough talent to be sure of a successful career in art. Not wanting to live out his days as a starving artist, and not wanting potential employers to perceive him as someone who is looking for a job only in order to pay the bills while pursuing an art career, Raymond created a decidedly business-oriented résumé.

The Solution. Raymond was lucky enough to have had two exceptional work experiences while in school. He worked for a large employment agency full-time for three summers, part-time during the first two years of college, and when home on vacations from college. He also worked for a large retail department store part-time while in college and full-time one summer. These experiences both involved management-type responsibilities. Since Raymond had enjoyed both jobs very much and since he had advanced in both organizations, he decided to capitalize on his experiences and seek employment in retail management or in human resources.

Raymond's résumé lets his work experiences do most of the "talking." They are positioned prominently, taking up more space than any other entries, and are described in detail. A potential employer reading these descriptions must conclude that Raymond is a person who can manage people and tasks and accomplish objectives. Raymond did not want to use an objective statement, because he felt he could draw attention to whichever experience was most relevant to the job he was applying for by means of a covering letter.

Although he was a studio art major, Raymond does not stress any of his art-related skills. In fact, he notes his major only in the last section of his résumé. His greatest strengths are in fact the skills he acquired in his two long-term work experiences, and Raymond sells these strengths very effectively.

Summary. Raymond's résumé highlights two very good work experiences and projects a person who can and will succeed in business. This art major will not be painted into a corner, and he will not be stereotyped. He will, however, be successful in his efforts to find a job that will get him started in a business career.

Typewritten using a Prestige Elite element. ➡

RAYMOND KRIEGER

3218 SE Woodstock Blvd.   182 Federal Ave.
Apartment 4   Apartment 32B
Portland, Oregon 97202   Los Angeles, California 90045
(302) 776-3195   (213) 823-6284

WORK EXPERIENCE

<u>Personnel Counselor</u>, Dynamic Personnel Resources, Inc., Los Angeles, CA
Interviewed applicants, initiated and developed employer contacts, visited client company operations, coordinated applicant and employer communications from initial contact to hiring. Specialized in clerical personnel.

Provided direct support for manager of clerical area--trained and supervised personnel counselors, maintained daily, weekly, and monthly individual and area performance records.

<u>Summers 1981-1983 and part-time as needed 1981-1983</u>

<u>Assistant Buyer/Salesperson</u>, I. Magnin, Portland, OR
Ordered merchandise, coordinated its arrival and transfer to departments, completed all paperwork involved in pricing and advertising, and supervised display of merchandise. Completed Junior Executive Training Program while full-time student. Promoted into program after six months as part-time salesperson.

As salesperson, assisted customers with selections, displayed merchandise, maintained inventory, and tabulated daily receipts.

<u>Summer 1984 and part-time 1983-present</u>

EXTRACURRICULAR ACTIVITIES

<u>Fund-Raising Volunteer</u>, Reed College Development Office, Portland, OR
Solicited alumni donations via telephone fund-raising drives.

<u>1983 and 1984</u>

<u>Kappa Sigma Fraternity</u>, Reed College, Portland, OR
Publicity Chairman--Promoted fraternity events using posters and flyers. Designed and created all promotional materials. Coordinated decorations at various functions.

<u>1982-1983</u>

<u>Greekspeak</u>, Reed College, Portland, OR
Editor--Organized, edited, and coordinated production of newsletter for fraternities and sororities.

<u>1981-1983</u>

INTERESTS

<u>Art</u>
Sketch and paint landscapes and portraits.
<u>Travel</u>
Traveled throughout western United States, Mexico, and Spain. Speak Spanish.

EDUCATIONAL BACKGROUND

<u>Reed College</u>, Portland, OR
Bachelor of Arts in Studio Art, May 1985
Minor in English

Patricia M. Lansing:
A Scientist Seeks a Setting

Special Features
- Targeted résumé without objective statement
- Highlights scientific experiences with carefully selected headings and boldface type
- Used for job search, graduate school applications, and grant proposals

The Problem. Patricia M. Lansing, a biology major, wanted to make use of her academic and extracurricular science activities to obtain an entry-level position with a scientific research organization, environmental protection organization, or laboratory. She had done a great deal but had received only tuition credit or room and board for her efforts. Patricia did not receive an hourly wage or salary for any of the activities listed, but her aim was to present herself as a goal-oriented person with notable qualifications, not just as a science major with many volunteer experiences in her background.

The Solution. Patricia's résumé reflects her desires clearly, but it does so without an objective statement. The largest section is the one labeled Scientific Experience. Here Patricia discusses all of her science-related experiences. The question of whether she was paid for any of this work is irrelevant. Potential employers will see Patricia as a person qualified to work in research-oriented environments. They will have no doubts that she is experienced, and that is what is most important.

Patricia has clearly done more than laboratory work. She has done independent research, been involved in the research efforts of others, taught college and high school students, and gained computer programming capabilities. All of these qualifications are presented effectively on her résumé.

In addition to forwarding her résumé, Patricia provides each prospective employer with a copy of her transcripts and synopses of some of her research papers. This supplemental information will no doubt increase her chances of being selected. Liberal arts graduates seeking employment in scientific settings should ex-

pect to be asked to provide additional materials such as transcripts, synopses, and letters of recommendation. These documents can be submitted with the résumé when first making contact with an employer or at a later time, perhaps after the interview.

The absence of an objective statement allows Patricia to use her résumé for purposes other than a job search. She may decide she wants to apply for admission to a doctoral program and for funding to continue her research. The résumé she developed is an ideal vehicle for presenting her background to graduate schools and funding agencies; it presents much of the needed information in a concise and organized fashion. Having the résumé at hand will allow Patricia to explore any of these options with very little extra effort.

Format and Layout. Patricia has developed a format that highlights her scientific experiences in various ways. As discussed, the largest section appears under the heading Scientific Experience. Patricia highlights the names of the organizations in each entry by having them set in capital letters. She sets off each activity in a similar way by using boldface type and having bullets set in front of each item. Potential employers reviewing this résumé can quickly orient themselves and pick out related experiences. Patricia also uses boldface italics to highlight the summary statements that appear at the end of the Scientific Experience section.

Typeset in Helvetica. ➡

PATRICIA M. LANSING

29 Campus Drive
Durham, NC 27706
Home: (919) 684-9729
Office: (919) 684-3300

4 Agerton Road
Augusta, GA 30909
(912) 736-8726

EDUCATION

DUKE UNIVERSITY   *Durham, NC*
- *A.B., June 1985*
- *Honors major in Biology   Overall GPA: 3.3   Biology GPA: 3.5*
- *Duke University Marching Band (1984-1985)*
- *Editor, Events Calendar (1984-1985)*
- *Delta Delta Delta Sorority (1982-1985)*

AUGUSTA SENIOR HIGH SCHOOL   *Augusta, GA*
- *Graduated 5th in class of 400, June 1981*
- *President, Biology Club (1979-1981)*
- *Nominated for Georgia Science Awards (1981)*

SCIENTIFIC EXPERIENCE

DUKE UNIVERSITY DEPARTMENT OF BIOLOGY   *Durham, NC*

- *Attended **Tropical Biology Study Program** in Puerto Rico (Summer 1984). Investigated aspects of terrestrial and marine ecology through lectures and field study. Originated hypotheses and researched and presented oral and written findings of group and individual projects.*
- *Received State of North Carolina grants to support **independent research on insect activities** (1983-1985). Designed and constructed original electronic equipment to quantify movement as related to temperature. Results used as a part of developing insect control strategy for Department of Agriculture.*
- ***Teaching Assistant** in Entomology (Summer 1983) and Botany (Spring 1982). Included laboratory instruction and field supervision, preparation and grading of examinations, and monitoring use of laboratory equipment.*
- ***Research Assistant** (1981-1983). Conducted chemical and biological experiments on pesticide potencies. Involved use of computers, sophisticated instruments, and advanced laboratory techniques.*

NATIONAL YOUTH SCIENCE CAMP   *Charleston, WV*
- ***Counselor** (Summer 1982). Taught seminars on botany and natural sciences.*
- *Selected as one of two students from Georgia to attend **six-week symposium on scientific topics** (Summer 1981). Chosen to return as counselor the following summer.*

UNITED STATES DEPARTMENT OF ENVIRONMENTAL PROTECTION   *Augusta, GA*
- *Selected member of Youth Conservation Corps (Summer 1980). Improved trails and controlled erosion in state parks.*

Can program in BASIC and COBOL. Experienced in variety of laboratory techniques and use of laboratory equipment.

Judson Marks:
Excellent Experience, No Direction

> **Special Features**
> - Highlights skills to downplay lack of focus
> - Detailed discussion of excellent work experiences
> - Use of word processor allows for objectives to be added as needed
> - Personalized stationery supplies graphic interest

The Problem. Judson Marks is a French major who has had excellent work experience yet lacks direction. He is unsure of what specific career field or job function would be right for him. After talking with a career counselor, assessing skills developed through previous work and extracurricular activities, and setting tentative job-search targets, Judson still had a problem. "I have narrowed down my areas of interest to six—international banking, marketing research, management information systems programming, manufacturing management, manufacturing purchasing, and consulting—but I can't narrow them down any further." Having so many different career interests made it difficult for Judson to decide on what type of résumé to use.

The Solution. To solve his problem, Judson decided it would be best to have his résumé typed on a word processor so that he could quickly and easily change his objective statement as needed. The sample résumé printed here has no objective. Not only can Judson add an objective statement at a later date, he can revise the Skills Overview section to support the target job as stated in the objective.

Most of Judson's résumé is taken up by the Skills Overview and Work Experience sections. These two segments are the heart of his résumé, for Judson's greatest assets come from the excellent experiences he has had over the summers. Judson first draws attention to the skills gained via these experiences, then provides detailed discussions of the responsibilities associated with each summer job. Judson also comments on the information that appears below these two major headings, but does not go into quite as much detail.

Judson can change objectives and redirect the Skills Overview to prepare for directed communication with prospective employers in specific fields as needed. Rewriting a résumé forces self-assessment and prompts continued research into potential job functions. Remember, the more you know about yourself and about the job you wish to have, the better able you'll be to communicate this knowledge in a résumé, covering letter, or interview.

Format and Layout. Judson's résumé is typed each time by a word processor with the particular objective and Skills Overview Judson needs for the job he is interested in at the time. Judson decided to order his own paper and have his name printed boldly in the upper left-hand corner. This gives his résumé a little flair and makes it easy to pick out. The body of the résumé itself is laid out in a fairly traditional, conservative way, so that overall, the résumé looks very businesslike. Judson gives only one address on his résumé since using the word processor enables him to change his address as necessary before he has a new version printed out.

Summary. For a person with excellent experience but no real direction, this approach to résumé writing is very effective. After Judson has done a little more research, he should be able to narrow down the possibilities a bit more. Six job-search target fields are probably too much to handle, even for someone as experienced as Judson.

Typeset in Century Schoolbook Condensed. ➡

JUDSON MARKS

117 Skinker Boulevard
St. Louis, MO 63130
(314) 889-6620

SKILLS OVERVIEW

Capable of organizing and coordinating ideas as well as people and working toward specific goals. Can assess situations to develop and implement problem-solving strategies.

Capable of researching and analyzing information for practical use, such as writing a computer program to increase efficiency of information retrieval and deciding which contractors to use for major and minor repairs to fraternity house.

Trained and motivated people to achieve maximum performance in work and academic environments. Able to communicate and work with people of all ages and backgrounds.

As House Manager developed and utilized strong management, leadership, and decision-making abilities. Supervised members, administered budgets, and maintained facilities.

As employee of Southwestern Bell was exposed to Marketing, Plant, and Revenue departments. Completed all assignments successfully. Developed special projects in addition to fulfilling responsibilities appearing on job descriptions.

WORK EXPERIENCE

SOUTHWESTERN BELL TELEPHONE COMPANY, St. Louis, MO

Division of Revenues: Economic Analyst   Summer 1984

Collected information to write a computer program (BASIC) that analyzed revenues by departments and by weekly, monthly, and quarterly time periods. Supervised and instructed employees who entered data into system. Consulted with managers in other regional departments in order to gather data for study dealing with costs in Traffic Services Department. Prepared manual to instruct keypunchers on data input procedures for Traffic Services study. Presented results of study in a report to Division Manager and Division Vice President.

Plant Department: Summer Trainee   Summer 1983

Recorded and filed customer repair tickets. Updated repair equipment records. Entered customer repair data into computer.

Marketing Department: Summer Trainee   Summer 1982

Assisted in forecasting department budget. Compiled and analyzed studies on use of WATS systems by small businesses. Researched potential customers/companies for marketing purposes. Reviewed employee work schedules and devised vacation replacement schedules. Reorganized filing systems.

EDUCATION

WASHINGTON UNIVERSITY   St. Louis, MO
Bachelor of Arts, anticipated June 1985   Major: French
Overall GPA: 3.25/4.0.

ACTIVITIES

PHI DELTA ALPHA FRATERNITY, Washington University

House Manager   1983-1985

Administered $5,000 annual budget. Assigned rooms to members living in the house. Billed members for room and board expenses. Supervised two full-time staff persons and two student assistants. Attended house executive board meetings and decided upon issues related to the house. Had total control over all maintenance and repairs decisions and allocations.

Communications Chairman   1984-1985

Informed fraternity members of university and house events.

Intramural Chairman   1983-1984

INTRAMURAL DEPARTMENT, Washington University

Referee and Scorekeeper   1982-1984

PROJECT MOTIVATION, St. Louis, MO

Tutor and Counselor   1980-1982

Tutored and counseled underprivileged children in two inner-city elementary schools.

REFERENCES

Available upon request.

Randee Sue Stemmons:
The Newsworthy Psychology Major

Special Feature
● Skills and Abilities section used with Objective draws attention to Randee's capabilities, not her major
---

The Problem. Randee Stemmons is one of many psychology majors who have no intentions of becoming a psychologist. She wishes to find employment as a journalist, either in print or broadcast news. But she has not majored in journalism, and she is aware that she will be competing with students who have done so.

The Solution. To show potential employers the qualifications she has to meet the responsibilities of an entry-level position in journalism, Randee developed two different résumés. The first (page 71) is relatively traditional in format and content, while the second (page 72) is somewhat unusual, taking the form of a brief news piece. The second serves as both résumé and writing sample.

Randee has had some experiences that were directly related to her job goals, and she naturally wanted to highlight them on her résumé. To do so she included a Skills and Abilities section in her basic résumé and discussed these attributes in more detail in her news-piece résumé. Randee has had courses in journalism, technical writing, creative writing, and research techniques. These are highlighted in both résumés. Randee's on-air experience with her university's radio station was limited (she became involved in the station only after focusing on her job-search target late in her senior year), but it was a valid experience and therefore appears in both résumés. Randee also cites experience she had with newspapers during her high school days, and, although it wasn't very extensive, it at least demonstrates her interest in the field of journalism.

Special Uses. Randee can use either résumé alone, depending on the employer, or she can use them as a package. The news-piece résumé is a bit unorthodox, and it could turn some conservative professionals off, but it is well written (Randee had a journalism professor

assist her in developing the piece), and it presents her strengths in a forceful, upbeat manner. Even if she doesn't use the news-piece résumé for all job applications, she can use a great deal of its content in covering letters and during interviews. Randee also developed a small portfolio that includes some letters-to-the-editor that had been published in her university newspaper, a few of the pieces she did for journalism and creative-writing classes, and some articles she wrote for her high school paper. In addition, Randee wrote a few samples of news copy about current events and had a tape recording made of her reporting the stories.

Format and Layout. Randee's basic résumé highlights her focus and qualifications by means of the Objective statement and the Skills and Abilities section. The news piece incorporates techniques like italics to highlight "quoted sources." Both résumés were typed and duplicated on high-quality paper to present a professional image.

Summary. Randee's résumés work for her because they project an image of someone who knows what will be expected of her in an entry-level position and who is confident of her ability to meet those expectations.

Typeset in Century Schoolbook. ➡

RANDEE SUE STEMMONS

Box 3987
North Texas State University
Denton, Texas 76203
(817) 563-2105

2323 Shady Glenn Drive
Apartment 1328-B
Dallas, Texas 75206
(214) 363-7643

OBJECTIVE

A position in the field of journalism involving research and reporting.

SKILLS AND ABILITIES

Strong written and verbal communications skills...on-air experience...command of research techniques required of journalistic and academic writing...course work in technical writing, creative writing, journalism, and research techniques...assertiveness...ability to work under pressure.

EDUCATION

North Texas State University, Denton, Texas.
Bachelor of Arts, December 1985. Major: Psychology. Minor: Art History.
Grade Point Average for the final three academic semesters: 3.75/4.0.
Dean's List: fall 1983, spring 1984, and fall 1984.

ACTIVITIES

KNTSU, North Texas State University (fall 1984). Disc jockey for student radio station. Presented music programming and read hourly news reports.
Denton School for Special Education, Denton, Texas (summer 1984 and part-time 1983-present). Volunteer Counselor. Assist counseling staff to implement educational and therapeutic programs to children and adults.
Residence Life Office, North Texas State University (fall 1982-present). Resident Assistant. Advise students on academic questions. Counsel students with personal problems. Act as liaison between students and Residence Life Office. Check students into dormitory rooms at the beginning of each semester and check students out of dormitory rooms at the end of each academic year. Take inventory of dormitories at the end of each academic year.
NTSU DAILY, North Texas State University (1981-present). Contributed numerous feature articles to student newspaper.
THE LION'S ROAR, Richardson High School, Richardson, Texas (1980-1981). Reporter. Contributed articles on various subjects. Specialized in sports.

REFERENCES

Richard C. Donner, Professor of English, (817) 563-2235.
Louise Ann Create, Professor of Psychology, (817) 563-2471.
Maryann McWhales, Director of Residence Life, (817) 563-5566.
(All are at North Texas State Unversity, Denton, Texas 76203.)

STUDENT SEEKS POSITION AS JOURNALIST

by Randee Sue Stemmons

After undertaking a thorough process of self-assessment and career research, Randee Sue Stemmons of 2323 Shady Glenn Drive, Apartment 1328-B, Dallas, Texas 75206, phone number (214) 363-7643, recently launched a determined effort to obtain employment in the field of journalism. Specifically, Ms. Stemmons is seeking a position involving research or reporting in broadcasting or newspaper journalism.

Randee will receive a Bachelor of Arts degree from North Texas State University in Denton, Texas, in December 1985. A psychology major and art history minor, Randee expresses confidence that her academic, extracurricular, and employment experiences have provided the skills and motivation required to become a successful journalist. When questioned about specific skills and motivations, Stemmons said,

> *"My course work in psychology and art history has taught me how to express myself verbally and in writing. I can do the research required to prepare a story or article. I can analyze questions from a scientific, behavioral, or artistic perspective. I am intensely curious about how people feel and act—what makes them tick. I am assertive—if I want to know something, I'll ask questions and find answers. Pressure is an everyday thing at school. I constantly work under the pressure of deadlines, sometimes working, 20-hour days on assignments."*

Comparing her background to that of a journalism major, Stemmons remarked,

> *"I have taken Scientific and Technical Writing, Creative Writing, Research Techniques, and Introduction to Journalism: Basic Writing. My transcript may not have all of the course titles a journalism major has, but I have many of the skills that a journalism major does. I can write effectively in synopsis and prose forms. My psychology courses have provided me with training in interview techniques, and I have had some on-air experience at my school's radio station."*

The past four years at NTSU have been more than courses, examinations, and term papers for Randee. She was a member of the residence-life staff for three years, a volunteer at the Denton School for Special Education for the past two, and has worked at the student radio station this fall. Learning-by-doing has been a theme in her education.

> *"I learned from all of my nonacademic experiences that listening and communicating are the keys to success. Listening allows someone to understand another person and the situation in which he or she is involved. Knowing how to translate listening into a written form is what journalism is all about. I have seen what listening and good communication can produce in an academic environment and in a therapeutic setting such as the school for special education. I want to share ideas and events with those who read printed media or with those who watch and listen to broadcast media."*

Randee is well aware that a search for a position in the field of journalism will not be easy. She knows that there are only a few jobs and a great many job seekers, and that only a select few are given opportunities to enter. Randee is a realist about her chances.

> *"I know it isn't going to be easy, especially since I majored in psychology and not in journalism or English, but I feel qualified and, most importantly, prepared. I have done a great deal of homework and thinking."*

She is nevertheless also optimistic about her chances for success.

> *"My commitment to finding a job is very strong. I am sure there is a person out there who will give me a chance to prove myself. I don't want to start out as an editor or on-air reporter. All I am looking for is an entry-level position. I want to proofread or write copy, research stories or articles, and assist in the production of stories. I want to have a chance to learn while I am performing what is expected of me. My portfolio may not be as full or sophisticated as a journalism major's, but it contains examples of the type of things I can do. It includes some of the articles I wrote for the Richardson High School newspaper, The Lion's Roar, and some of the letters-to-the-editor I had published in the North Texas State University Daily. I have also included some synopses of research papers I have written. All I want is a chance to show these to someone and an opportunity to tell someone why I want to be a journalist and how my experiences have prepared me to be a good journalist."*

Randee Stemmons is set on finding a job in journalism, and she asks for a chance. If determination and hard work are what make successful job seekers and successful journalists, Randee meets those requirements. *"She has been successful, and will continue to be successful,"* is what Richard C. Donner, Professor of English at North Texas State University, (817) 563-2235; Louise Ann Create, Professor of Psychology, (817) 563-2471; and Maryann McWhales, Director of Residence Life, (817) 563-5566, echoed when questioned about Randee. Each of these individuals said that they would recommend her highly for positions in journalism and that they would welcome inquiries from employers seeking information on Randee's abilities.

If one believes what others say about Randee Sue Stemmons and what Randee has to say about herself, she will no doubt be an excellent journalist someday.

Howard M. Stevens:
Ordinary Guy Does Not Want an Ordinary Résumé

Special Features
- Traditional layout and graphics used to create professional image
- Internship heading highlights most important experience

The Problem. Howard M. Stevens, a social science major, thinks of himself as just an ordinary guy. Although Howard has had some interesting experiences, most notably an internship with a public television station, he did not have the confidence or enthusiasm required to create an effective résumé or mount an aggressive job search. After receiving some simple suggestions from a career counselor concerning ways to highlight important information on his résumé, Howard seemed to perk up. The résumé Howard devised not only illustrates a good approach to résumé writing, but it reflects his growing self-confidence.

If Howard receives additional career counseling focused on researching potential career fields, he will become even more confident of his abilities and of his qualifications for employment. With a job goal in mind, Howard can rework the résumé by adding an Objective statement and, perhaps, some form of summary of skills. For now, the résumé as it appears can be used for many purposes, for researching employment opportunities by means of informational interviews as well as for applying for specific jobs.

The Solution. Howard was at first concerned that he wouldn't be able to fill up a page with pertinent information. After being told by a counselor that it is not the length of the résumé but the content, the format, and, most importantly, what one does with the résumé that count, Howard relaxed and was finally able to write a very good first draft. In this draft Howard highlighted what he believed was his most important experience while in school (next to playing varsity basketball!). This was his internship with a public television

station. He placed this entry in a prominent position and used a special heading to make it stand out.

Initial career research, including a number of informational interviews, has led Howard to consider applying for jobs as a researcher with a federal, city, or state agency; with an elected official; or with a television or radio station. Howard came to realize that his internship experience and course work provided him with a background that could be applied in any of these target fields. He therefore styled his résumé to attract the attention of employers in these specific areas.

Format and Layout. Howard's résumé is very traditional in its appearance and layout. It uses basic headings to present experiences and capitalization to highlight major headings. Liberal spacing was used between separate elements of the résumé to make the document appear a bit fuller than it really is and to project a very businesslike image. Howard used matching stationery and envelopes to create a thoroughly professional presentation.

Summary. Howard sought the advice of professional career counselors, which resulted in his being able to zero in on several job-target fields that have real potential for him. He is very pleased with his résumé—finally having a completed document in hand seems to have made life a lot easier—and he is now very optimistic about his chances for success. Howard is not really as ordinary as he thought. He had been suffering from the lack of self-confidence that too many liberal arts graduates have at first, but with this résumé he has taken a first step, a major step, toward job-search success.

HOWARD M. STEVENS _____

P.O. Box 239
Creighton University
Omaha, Nebraska 68178
(402) 448-7895

EDUCATION _____

Creighton University, Omaha, Nebraska.
<u>Bachelor of Arts in Social Science</u>, expected May 1985.

Course work included: Legislative Process, Sociological Research
   Techniques, Practical Electoral Politics, The Media and the Law,
   Introduction to Journalism.

INTERNSHIP _____

Nebraska Public Television, spring and fall 1984.

Researched information for investigative report on housing
discrimination in Lincoln and Omaha as part of social science and
political science courses. Did voice-overs for portions of
production. Wrote term paper on issues of media's impact on
legislative process.

ACTIVITIES _____

Creighton University Varsity Basketball, 1981-1985.

Kappa Kappa Kappa Fraternity, 1982-1985.

Nebraska Public Television, 1984-1985.

Answered phones during membership and fund-raising drives.

Political Campaigns, 1984.

Campaigned door-to-door and on the telephone for congressional and
gubernatorial candidates.

EXPERIENCE _____

Omaha Credit Collection Agency, summers, 1984 and 1982.

Collected overdue installment accounts and counseled customers on
suitable repayment plans.

Creighton University Athletic Department, part-time 1983-1985.

Opened and closed gym and maintained locker room areas.

Creighton University Alumni Memorial Library, summer 1983.

Checked out and restacked books.

REFERENCES _____

A placement file, including letters of recommendation, is available upon
request from the Creighton University Office of Career Planning and
Placement, Lower Becker Hall, Room 38, Omaha, Nebraska 68178.

Jay B. Stuart:
Pre-Med Retread—Life After Rejection

Special Features
- Basic résumé for variety of job-search options
- Can be used for reapplication to med school

The Problem. Jay B. Stuart was a chemistry major who applied to medical school and didn't get in. He had good grades (a 3.0 GPA) and strong work and extracurricular experiences, but he didn't have exactly what the schools he applied to were looking for. After dealing with the emotional effects of rejection and coming to terms with the fact that he had to explore other options, Jay sought the assistance of his professors and a career counselor. After digesting all of the advice he received and doing a great deal of soul-searching, Jay decided that he would do something related to the field of medicine for a year or two and then reapply to medical school. Because Jay was realistic enough to know that he might not be admitted to med school when he re-applied and because he wanted to continue to consider workable alternative careers, he decided to start his first job hunt with a broad, multipurpose résumé.

The Solution. Because the number of possible careers in medicine and health-related fields is so large, Jay felt most comfortable with a résumé that did not have an objective statement. He wanted to be able to stress his particular strengths, as appropriate, in covering letters or during interviews. For example, if he were applying for a laboratory job, he would include in his letter details about the many lab courses he had taken and highlight the laboratory techniques he was familiar with. For positions in hospital administration or patient services, Jay might choose to elaborate on the administrative and organizational skills he included under the Activities heading.

Jay's academic, extracurricular, and employment experiences have left him with some very valuable skills. Because he is unsure about how and where he might apply these skills and because he wants to keep his options open, Jay prefers a résumé that could be used to apply for jobs in a number of different medical and health-related fields.

Special Uses. Jay's résumé is a very good basic document that can be reworked in a number of ways. If Jay does reapply to medical school, an updated version of the résumé, stressing scientific course work and research experience could be used to support his candidacy. If continued exploration of careers leads Jay to seek jobs outside of the field of medicine, his résumé could easily be reworked to emphasize general skills.

Format and Layout. Jay typed his résumé, using traditional major headings and a chronological listing. It presents a very good image and is appropriate for the variety of employers that Jay will contact.

Summary. After having invested so much time and energy and emotion into applying to medical school and being rejected, Jay wants to redirect his efforts at obtaining the very best alternative job possible. Although unsure of exactly what this job will be, he is undertaking all of the activities required to gain focus and carry out a successful job search. For this pre-med retread, life after med school rejection will be successful.

JAY B. STUART

Present Address   Home Address
3264 Maple   48 Dix Hills Road
Clinton, New York   13323   Dix Hills, New York   11746
(315)   853-9753   (516)   644-8639

EDUCATION

Hamilton College, Clinton, NY
Candidate for A.B., June 1985
Chemistry major

Additional course work in economics, statistics, computer
science (BASIC), and psychology

Half Hollow Hills High School West, Dix Hills, NY
Graduated June 1981, top 10% of the class

ACTIVITIES

Hamilton College Community Services Committee
Governing Board (1982-1984)
Carried out administrative functions of organization.
Developed budget proposal, presented budget request
to administration, and administered approved budget.

Big Brother/Big Sister Program (1982-1985)
Cochairperson (1984-1985)
Organized program-wide events, recruited new members,
and matched pairs.
Big Brother to local underprivileged youth (1982-1985)

Sigma Nu Fraternity (1982-1985)

Half Hollow Hills Blood Drive
Coordinator (1979-1981)
Chaired committee that administered school blood drives.
Selected sites, recruited donors, and handled relations
with Red Cross.

WORK EXPERIENCE

Lenox Hill Hospital, New York, NY
Supervisor, Summer Youth Employment Program (summer 1984)
Supervised forty youths who served as volunteers in all areas
of hospital, including emergency room, pharmacy, and wards.
Assigned weekly responsibilities, oversaw completion of
assignments, interacted with hospital staff and
administration, and dealt with concerns of program
participants.

University of Southern California Medical School, Los Angeles, CA
Research Assistant (summer 1983)
Carried out neurophysiological experiments on animals. Analyzed
data and did library research. Proofread manuscripts.

Camp Merrimac, Contoocook, NH
Lifeguard and counselor (summers 1982 and 1981)

Lois Timstead:
Vita to Résumé:
Rejecting a Gypsy Scholar's Life

Special Features
- A functional résumé for a job search outside of academia
- Skills and Qualifications section, appearing first, highlights greatest strengths

The Problem. After over 17 years in higher education—eight as a student and over ten as a full-time teacher—Lois decided it was time to seek opportunities outside of academia. To do this, she first of all had to change her curriculum vitae into a résumé.

Lois had prepared herself for life as a college professor. After completing work for a Ph.D. from Cornell, Lois received an appointment at SUNY Binghamton. She was delighted to be working in New York State and dreamed of being granted tenure and staying forever. Forever turned out to be only three years, however. Denied an advancement, Lois decided to move to Oregon for a change of life-style and climate. The climate was indeed different, but her working life-style was too much the same. Having been unable to obtain an appointment at the University of Oregon, Lois settled for a position on the faculty of a community college. Sometime later, Lois was finally granted a position as visiting lecturer at the University of Oregon. After fulfilling the responsibilities of both jobs for several months, Lois began to think about whether she wanted to work this hard, continuing down a path she had walked before without any assurances that it would lead to the security she sought. But as an ex-teacher and a Ph.D. who could not find tenure, Lois was not certain she could present herself to an employer as someone worth hiring.

The Solution. After Lois sat down and worked on a skills flowchart and functional résumé, she realized that she really did have a great deal to offer potential employers. Lois decided to start searching for opportunities to use her foreign-language skills and knowledge of foreign countries and cultures. Lois was soon confident that her talents could be applied to the business world, and she became convinced that her skills as a free-lance translator and interpreter were marketable ones.

Format and Layout. Lois chose to write a functional résumé to replace her curriculum vitae and to highlight her skills. A curriculum vitae, sometimes called a "vita" or "c.v.," is a complete and thorough documentation of all academic experiences; it normally includes listings of education and employment, publications and presentations, and involvements in associations and committees. The résumé is a briefer, more functional document used to communicate with nonacademic employers.

Lois had her résumé typeset to project a businesslike image. She had earlier used a chronological approach on her vita but found it would be more effective to use a functional approach on her résumé, to both downplay her academic past and highlight the skills she has to offer. The Skills and Qualifications section sets the tone of the résumé and presents Lois as a person who has much to offer an organization involved in international business. Note that Lois summarized her teaching and writing experience and elaborated on her free-lance translating and interpreting and her involvement on various committees.

Summary. Having decided she does not want the life of a gypsy scholar, Lois developed a résumé that can be used to help her find the security as well as the challenges and rewards she seeks. Using this functional, efficient résumé, Lois should have no trouble finding an excellent job outside of the academic world.

LOIS TIMSTEAD

53 Arrowsmith Road
Eugene, Oregon 97402

Home (503) 686-3221
Work (503) 686-3558

SKILLS AND QUALIFICATIONS

FLUENT IN SPANISH AND PORTUGUESE, CONVERSANT IN ITALIAN.
- Can translate business documents, reports, and correspondence.
- Can interpret for individuals or groups.
- Can develop written materials—brochures, advertisements, reports, and letters.
- Can teach introductory, intermediate, and advanced levels of conversation to individuals or groups.

KNOWLEDGEABLE OF FOREIGN COUNTRIES, CULTURES, AND POLITICAL SYSTEMS.
- Can coordinate travel arrangements to foreign countries; special knowledge of Central America, South America, Mexico, and the Caribbean.
- Can act as guide for individuals or groups traveling to foreign countries and as host to foreign visitors.
- Can educate individuals involved in international business about cultural and political issues.

EXPERIENCED IN COORDINATING EVENTS AND WORKING WITH COMMITTEES.
- Can develop strategies to reach goals.
- Can coordinate all aspects of meetings and conferences.
- Can make decisions and delegate responsibility and supervise and judge the performance of others.

EXPERIENCE

FREE-LANCE TRANSLATOR AND INTERPRETER   1974-present

Have translated business documents and personal correspondence and have served as interpreter for numerous individuals and groups. Clients have included banks, travel agencies, manufacturers, retail stores, and social service agencies.

TEACHER AND WRITER   1975-present

Have taught Spanish and Portuguese language and literature at the University of Oregon (1984-present); Lane Community College (1982-present); State University of New York at Binghamton (1979-1982); and Cornell University (1975-1979). Have edited a textbook and written numerous articles.

EDUCATION

CORNELL UNIVERSITY, Ithaca, New York   1973-1979

Ph.D. Major Field: 20th-century Spanish-American literature.

UNIVERSITY OF WISCONSIN–MADISON, Madison, Wisconsin   1972-1973

M.A. Concentration: Ibero-American Studies. Minor: Portuguese.

STATE UNIVERSITY OF NEW YORK AT ALBANY, Albany, New York   1968-1972

B.A. Major: Latin American Studies. Minor: Spanish literature and language.

COMMITTEES AND ACTIVITIES

EXECUTIVE COMMITTEE OF ASSOCIATION OF CARIBBEAN STUDIES   1979-1981

Coordinated travel arrangements and accommodations for conferences in Havana, Cuba, and Nassau, Bahamas. Was responsible for securing facilities and supervising efforts of others at conference sites as well as negotiating with government officials. Each conference lasted four days and involved over 300 participants.

EXECUTIVE COMMITTEE OF THE FACULTY   1980-1981

Elected to serve on committee dealing with various academic and administrative issues, including tenure and curriculum, at State University of New York at Binghamton.

FACULTY COMMITTEE ON ADMISSIONS   1979-1981

Served on committee involved in admissions process at State University of New York at Binghamton.

REFERENCES

Available upon request.

Carol P. Wallace:
Leaving the Mental Health Field
for Peace of Mind

> **Special Features**
> - Objective highlights skills that are transferable from one field to another
> - Résumé shows the value of a mental health worker to business employer

The Problem. An undergraduate psychology major and holder of a Master of Arts degree in social and organizational psychology, Carol P. Wallace wants and needs a change. After working in a mental health setting for ten years, Carol is suffering from burnout. She wants to enter the business world to obtain such tangible rewards as money and steady advancement, but she is not exactly sure where she wants to work or in what capacity. Carol is absolutely certain she wants to make a change and can discuss for hours the reasons she is tired of working within the stressful environment of a psychiatric treatment facility. She feels she must make a change for her own peace of mind.

The Solution. Carol decided she needed a résumé that would project her motivation and her considerable skills (not her emotions!) to a potential employer. In order to decide which experiences to list, she began by making a careful assessment of skills. A review of her academic and employment experiences revealed several clearly definable skills areas that would be of interest to potential employers. Carol highlights these areas at the very beginning of the résumé under the heading Professional Objective, detailing her skills in three separate paragraphs labeled Management, Research and Evaluation, and Human Resources and Counseling. Carol can use this résumé effectively to respond to advertisements for specific job openings or to present to potential career advisers when requesting an informational interview.

By going through the process of assessing her skills and interests, which is required of anyone who hopes to write an effective résumé, Carol gained a greater awareness of the qualities she has to offer an employer. Having completed the résumé, she now feels that her job search has really begun. Carol can now go from talking about looking for a new job to taking action, to taking real steps toward her goal. As her job search continues and as increased knowledge of potential career fields results in more clearly focused job targets, Carol can revise her résumé by changing the Professional Objective—by replacing "business setting" with the name of the specific field or job she seeks—and by rephrasing the skill areas to reflect knowledge of the skills required for that specific field or job.

Format and Layout. Carol's résumé presents a person who has nothing to hide. She presents her academic background and experience, which are very much slanted to mental health/ psychology-related areas. She also communicates the fact that she is now ready to apply her skills in other fields by projecting her potential to employers by means of the Professional Objective section at the head of the résumé.

Summary. Carol's résumé will help her make the transition from her present field of employment to another. Completing the résumé was the first of many job-search activities that transformed Carol into a dynamic job seeker who catches the attention of employers in a wide range of fields. The fact that Carol is able to present her qualifications in terms of three skills areas rather than in terms of field-specific work experiences alone allows her to try her résumé out on recruiters from several different industries. Carol has a great deal more to do before her job search will end, but her résumé has gotten her off to a very good start.

Typewritten using a Letter Gothic element. ➡

CAROL P. WALLACE

38 Calle Buena
Tucson, Arizona 85715
(602) 625-0735

PROFESSIONAL OBJECTIVE

A position in a business setting utilizing the following skills:

MANAGEMENT - Supervisory responsibilities at Shadylawn involve management of staff, including scheduling, making evaluations, and hiring. Monitor use of all facilities and equipment and maintain detailed records.

RESEARCH AND EVALUATION - Course work in statistics, math, research design, and psychological testing. Completed master's thesis involving original hypothesis and research design. Gained experience in test administration and interpretation at Arizona Rehabilitation Commission. At Shadylawn develop written treatment plans for patients and maintain progress records.

HUMAN RESOURCES AND COUNSELING - Major academic training in psychology. All paid professional experiences involved working in a psychological services capacity. Have developed individual and group counseling skills. Capable of motivating staff to carry out treatment plans and maintaining high morale in stressful settings. While at Tucson Community College gained experience in academic and vocational counseling and cotaught a workshop for career changers.

EXPERIENCE

SHADYLAWN PSYCHIATRIC HOSPITAL, Tucson, AZ

* Area Supervisor/Mental Health Worker - January 1978--present.

* Psychiatric Aide - June 1976--January 1978.

TUCSON COMMUNITY COLLEGE, Tucson, AZ

* Counseling Center Intern - September 1976--June 1977, part-time while student.

ARIZONA REHABILITATION COMMISSION

* Psychological Assistant - December 1975--May 1976.

EDUCATION

UNIVERSITY OF ARIZONA, Tucson, AZ

* Master of Arts - Social and Organizational Psychology, August 1977. Emphasis on deviant behavior, counseling techniques, theories of social psychology, and research methods. Cumulative Grade Point Average: 3.4/4.0.

* Bachelor of Arts - Psychology, June 1975. Emphasis on experimental psychology and research design. Minor, Sociology. Cumulative Grade Point Average: 3.3/4.0.

REFERENCES

References, including letters of recommendation, are available upon request.

Nell Woodward:
A Major and a Résumé, Both Visual Studies

Special Features
- A targeted résumé that demonstrates the creativity that is associated with Nell's job-search goal
- Unique format and graphics

The Problem. Because she had no directly related experiences other than academic course work and a job in the art library, Nell decided that a few years in the field, working in drafting or in some other entry-level capacity, was what she needed. She created a résumé that would attract the attention of potential employers because of its unique format and graphics.

The Solution. Nell Woodward knew from the time she chose her major—visual studies—that she wanted to pursue a career in architecture. Tired of academics at the end of her senior year, Nell decided that she would rather get some practical training than go right on to a master's program in architecture. She therefore set her sights on an entry-level position with an architectural firm. Both the content and the format of Nell's résumé communicate her goals to potential employers: her statement of objective tells them exactly what she wants to do, and the résumé's creative design and layout demonstrate something of her artistic talents.

Format and Layout. Nell decided to have her résumé typeset, using a bold, artistic type style for major headings and a more conservative style for the content. When Nell sends her résumé to employers, she folds it accordian style, covering up everything but her name, addresses, and the Objective, Employment, Education, and Portfolio and References headings. Only when the flyer is opened up are the details under each heading revealed.

Summary. Nell's résumé would not be appropriate for a position with a bank, but it is very well-suited to the fields Nell is interested in. It presents information clearly and at the same time demonstrates her artistic style and design abilities.

NELL WOODWARD

Box 345
University of Massachusetts
Amherst, MA 01003
(413) 545-8635

34 King Arthur Court
Palo Alto, CA 94303
(415) 322-5445

An entry-level position with an architectural firm utilizing education and experience in architecture and visual studies.

EMPLOYMENT

YOUTH ENTERPRISES   Palo Alto, CA
Supervisor/Manager, January 1984–March 1984.
Supervised a group of high school students involved in recycling project. Responsible for accounts management and all public relations efforts.

GEMCO STORES   Mountain View, CA
Sales Clerk, September 1983–December 1983.
Performed sales, cashier, and stock duties. Ordered and maintained inventory for two departments of large retail department store.

EDUCATION

UNIVERSITY OF MASSACHUSETTS   Amherst, MA
Candidate for B.A., June 1985.
Major: Visual Studies with concentration in Architecture.
Course work in History of Architecture, Architectural Design, Urban Design, Computer
   Graphics, Physics, Engineering, and Drawing.
Activities: Director of Student Advertising Committee
           Member of Equestrian Team
           Participant in Foreign Study Program in Florence, Italy
           Freshman Adviser

UNIVERSITY LIBRARY, University of Massachusetts   Amherst, MA
Student Assistant to Art Librarian, September 1981–June 1985.
Responsible for circulation of all art journals and reserve materials and in-depth research for professors in Art Department.

PORTFOLIO AND REFERENCES

Complete portfolio of works and references are available upon request.

Stacey York:
The Past and Future Journalist, Perhaps

Special Features
- Two résumés used to expand job-search possibilities
- Chronological and functional résumés allow a job seeker with strong experiences in particular fields to present herself as well rounded and flexible

The Problem. An English literature major and psychology minor, Stacey is a person who seems to have done it all, but she is unsure of what she wants to do next. Much of her past extracurricular, academic, and work experience has been related to journalism, yet she is not convinced that she would like her first postgraduation job to be in journalism. Research of potential entry-level opportunities expanded her list of tentative job targets to include a number of fields outside of communications. Stacey decided she would like to interview for jobs in the following areas: advertising, broadcasting, consulting, book publishing, and magazine publishing; she also thinks she might enjoy writing speeches and/or doing administrative work for a Congressman or Senator.

Because she does in fact have a great deal to offer, Stacey can afford to approach the job hunt with a "grocery-store mentality" and shop around from employer to employer for a while. Because she did not want to keep track of six different résumés, Stacey developed two résumés that could communicate many things to many different employers.

The Solution. The use of a chronological résumé and a functional résumé titled Summary of Skills gives Stacey the flexibility she needs for her multidirectional job search. Both résumés effectively document many of her past experiences. Refer to Stacey's Chronological Flowchart on pages 15 to 19 and note that Stacey chose to document different experiences on each résumé; she did not include everything on both.

Stacey felt that her chronological résumé would not best present the breadth of her skills and experiences to employers in fields other than retailing or communications, so she created a functional résumé to use in other instances. The functional résumé best presents the broad range of skills that Stacey has to offer.

Special Uses. Stacey could, if she wishes, develop supplemental pages with summaries of skills for each of her job goals, and then create targeted functional résumés with stated objectives. This would allow her to highlight field-specific skills and use headings that do not appear on her general Summary of Skills. Specific skills identified in Stacey's Skills Flowchart and Job-Target Chart could be highlighted as appropriate on the targeted functional résumés.

Summary. Both versions of Stacey's résumé communicate the fact that she is accomplished in many different areas; the arrangement of the information and professional layout of the résumés testify to the fact that Stacey is a person who can make an attractive and effective presentation. Stacey's résumés give the clear impression that she will be able to apply her multidimensional talents—her Liberal Arts Power—to any challenge placed before her and that she will succeed!

Typewritten using a Letter Gothic element. ➡

STACEY YORK

Stanford University   349 Ridgewood Road
Post Office Box 783   Maplewood, New Jersey 07040
Stanford, California 94305   (201) 763-5894
(415) 498-8362

EDUCATION   STANFORD UNIVERSITY, Stanford, CA
                 Candidate for A.B. degree in June 1985.
                 GPA as of fall 1983 3.2 (out of a possible 4.0).
                 Major in English literature. Minor in psychology.

                 Participated in Stanford-in-France Program in Nice, France.
                 Member of Stanford Women's Crew. Editor STANFORD CREW NOTES.
                 Member of Alpha Chi Omega Sorority. Rush Co-Chairwoman and
                 Panhellenic Society Representative. Reporter for THE STANFORD
                 DAILY student newspaper.

                 COLUMBIA HIGH SCHOOL, Maplewood, NJ
                 Graduated in June 1981.
                 Ranked in top 10% of class.

                 National Honor Society.
                 Junior Class Secretary.
                 Editor of yearbook.

EXPERIENCE   STANFORD SPORTS INFORMATION OFFICE, Stanford, CA
                 ADMINISTRATIVE INTERN, spring 1983 to present
                 Reported on all Stanford sports events. Managed post-game
                 football pressbox operations for Stanford games and for
                 East-West Shrine games. Published feature stories about
                 Stanford athletes. Assisted in development of press guides
                 and programs. Wrote press releases.

                 FOOTBALL STATISTICIAN, fall 1984 and fall 1983.
                 Compiled statistics. Wrote game summaries and weekly reports.

                 MOBIL OIL CORPORATION, New York, NY
                 PUBLIC RELATIONS INTERN, summer 1984.
                 Researched information for Mobil's Op-Ed advertisements,
                 "Observations" columns, and special publications. Proofread
                 copy and checked facts. Replied to reader correspondence.
                 Coordinated Mobil School Visitation Program.

                 PALO ALTO HILTON INN, Palo Alto, CA
                 HOSTESS AND WAITRESS, summer 1983.

                 BAMBERGER'S DEPARTMENT STORE, Livingston, NJ
                 SALESPERSON, winter 1983 and summer 1982.

                 SUPERVISOR/SALESPERSON, fall 1979 to summer 1981.
                 Supervised salespersons, completed nightly closings, and
                 maintained various departments in manager's absence. Rotated
                 throughout store as needed. Youngest supervisor in store.

INTERESTS   Enjoy playing the piano and guitar, oil and acrylic painting.
                 Avid bicyclist. Have traveled in Europe and throughout the
                 western United States.

                 References available upon request.

```
STACEY YORK--Summary of Skills

        Stanford University                              349 Ridgewood Road
        Post Office Box 783                      Maplewood, New Jersey  07040
        Stanford, California  94305                       (201) 763-5894
        (415) 498-8362
```

OBJECTIVE   A position utilizing the skills acquired in the experiences outlined below.

WRITING
- Reported on sports events for THE STANFORD DAILY.
- Published feature stories for Stanford athletic programs and Bay Area newspapers.
- Currently working on a novel for independent study English course.

Samples of work available upon request.

RESEARCH
- Researched Mobil Oil Corporation's Op-Ed advertisements, "Observations" columns, and special publications.
- Updated statistical information for Stanford University football brochures and programs.
- Initiated independent study survey of students' opinions of the Stanford Honor Code. Presented results in videotape presentation.
- Conducted survey of passengers using Stanford shuttle bus system utilizing on-the-spot interviewing and questionnaires.

ORGANIZATION AND MANAGEMENT
- Edited STANFORD CREW NOTES. In charge of copy, layout, and circulation for monthly publication dealing with men's and women's crew.
- Student Liaison Officer for Stanford Alumni Club of Northern New Jersey. Coordinated activities for prospective students from northern New Jersey at Alumni Club events. Represented Stanford at college nights. Corresponded with applicants from northern New Jersey. Greeted and hosted visitors from northern New Jersey during stays at Stanford.
- Supervised salespersons and managed various departments as supervisor/salesperson at Bamberger's department store.
- Coordinated visits of over 25 schools (over 2,000 students) to Mobil Oil Corporation's world headquarters for Mobil's School Visitation Program.

CREATIVITY
- Studied piano for 10 years; additional training in guitar and voice.
- Performed in high school dramatic productions.
- Paint with oils and acrylics.

EDUCATION   STANFORD UNIVERSITY, A.B., June 1985
Major: English literature. Minor: psychology. GPA: 3.2/4.0.

EXPERIENCE   STANFORD SPORTS INFORMATION OFFICE, Administrative Intern (spring 1983-present), Football Statistician (fall 1984 and fall 1983).
MOBIL OIL CORPORATION, Public Relations Intern (summer 1984).
PALO ALTO HILTON INN, Hostess and Waitress (summer 1983).
BAMBERGER'S DEPARTMENT STORE, Salesperson (winter 1983 and summer 1982), Supervisor/Salesperson (fall 1979-summer 1981).

Writing Your Résumé

Now that you have taken stock of your skills, reviewed the sample résumés, and focused in on three or four job targets, you are prepared to actually write your résumé. There are of course many ways to write a résumé, and there are many topics that can be included in one. You will have to decide which topics are appropriate for *your* résumé in accordance with your objectives, your background, and other factors. The order in which topics appear on a résumé is also variable. By ordering material in a particular way, you highlight the information that you judge to be of most importance.

The sample résumés that appear in this book illustrate many ways to organize a résumé. To help you decide which topics will be appropriate for your résumé, a brief discussion of possible topics follows.

One of the most important decisions you must make at the outset is whether or not to include a statement describing your career goal.

The Contents

IDENTIFYING INFORMATION

Your name, address, and telephone number should be placed in a prominent position, usually at the top of the résumé. Some students give a permanent address and a school address, if both will be used during the job search. If your address or phone number changes while you are looking for a job, it is important that you correct and reprint your résumé and send follow-up letters announcing the change to those people you have already contacted.

OBJECTIVE

You may include a statement describing your career goal, job target, or reason for using the résumé. This is not appropriate for all résumés or all job seekers. One of the most important decisions you must make concerning the content of your résumé is whether or not to include a statement of this type.

Stating an objective tells potential employers that you are headed in a certain direction, informs them of your reasons for making contact, and serves as a focal point from which they can review and analyze the remainder of the résumé. The objective does not necessarily limit you or prevent the potential employer from considering you for positions other than those stated, but it does indicate that you have preferences. Some employers will not consider you for positions other than those specified in your statement of goals, but through follow-up contacts you can encourage them to do so.

Those job seekers who possess clear goals will want to present them on their résumé. Those who are considering more than one professional goal may develop more than one résumé, each presenting a different objective. Job seekers who are unsure of their career goals may develop a résumé without a statement of objective. But they can, and must, communicate a sense of direction in other ways. Covering letters and such documents as a Summary of Qualifications, which are distributed along with the résumé (and which are illustrated later in this book), can serve this purpose.

Do not be afraid to state an objective. Doing so does not mean making a lifelong commitment to a particular job or field. And a well-written objective can be very useful in communicating goals and qualifications. If you do use one, make sure that it tells potential employers clearly what you want to do, using job titles and functional descriptions that are recognizable and that reflect your knowledge of the areas in which you are seeking employment. A vaguely worded objective can do more harm than good.

Activities and exercises appearing in the section called Steps to Writing Your Résumé are designed to help you define your career goals.

Remember that a vaguely worded objective can do more harm than good.

EDUCATION

Include undergraduate and graduate study, as well as foreign study and special academic programs. Degrees, institutions and their locations, dates graduated or dates attended, and majors and minors can be included. As with all entries on a résumé, you decide what to include. Academic course work and areas of academic emphasis, if they are related to your objective, may be included. Scholarships, honor society memberships, special awards, and grade point averages can also be mentioned. You may wish to give your GPA in your major or some other specific academic area in addition to or instead of your cumulative GPA. Some students give their averages for a certain period of time, such as their junior and senior years, if this information is more flattering. Education can be presented under special headings, such as Science Education, Computer Education, or Business-related Education, which allows the job seeker to group related experiences and give his or her résumé a particular focus.

EXPERIENCE

List full-time and part-time jobs, as well as volunteer work, internships, externships, and other career-related experiences. State the titles you held and the names of the organizations and describe the experiences in active, skills-oriented terms. Whenever possible, mention specific accomplishments. A common way of presenting this information is in reverse chronological order. You can also group related experiences together under special titles, such as Counseling Experience, Computer Experience, or Business Experience.

Include specific accomplishments, emphasize skills, and use action verbs when describing your experiences.

EXTRACURRICULAR AND COMMUNITY ACTIVITIES

Give the names of organizations and, if appropriate, offices held, accomplishments, and special projects. Your description of your activities should make potential employers aware of the skills you have acquired through them.

If your activities associated with a club, school group, or community organization are directly related to the career or job you want, you may describe them under an Experience heading instead of under Activities. Whether you received payment for your contributions of time and energy should not determine where you describe it on your résumé. The nature of your responsibilities and their relationship to your career goals should be the deciding factors.

Commenting on the importance of extracurricular activities from the perspective of one who hires many college graduates, Russ Dunham, District Manager, Procter & Gamble, says: "We look for people who set goals for themselves and then set specific plans to reach those goals. We have found that students who have been actively involved in a number of activities while in college have already dealt with the problem solving and priority setting which are important in our field."

SPECIAL CATEGORIES

Almost anything can be treated as a special category on a résumé. Presenting information under its own heading is a good way of highlighting it. The categories outlined below—Skills, Qualifications, Languages, and Computer Languages—are the most common.

Other special headings might include Supervisory Experience, Finance Background, Teaching Activities, or Travel and International Experience. You can use such special categories to support your Objective and project a sense of direction to employers. The Objective focuses the attention of the potential employer on a particular job, while the information you give in special categories documents and explains the qualifications you have for that job.

• Skills

List and discuss the skills you possess that can be used on the job. Document your skills with examples of work, activities, and educational experiences. Functional résumés, which are discussed later, make particularly prominent use of skills headings, but other types of résumés can have them too.

• Qualifications

You can use a Qualifications section to summarize your skills, education, character, and motivation in a way that shows how they qualify you for the employment you seek.

• Languages

List foreign languages you know and briefly describe your level of fluency in each.

• Computer Languages

Be sure to list any computer languages you know and to indicate your level of expertise for each of them. This information can be included with a summary of college course work or highlighted under a separate heading.

INTERESTS

If you wish, you may include a few informal statements about your travel experiences, hobbies, and interests in order to tell prospective employers a bit about the "nonbusiness" aspects of your background. It is best to leave this information off the résumé if you need space for more important information. If you have acquired special skills as a result of pursuing your interests, discuss these skills under a special heading, rather than under Interests, to ensure that employers will read this information.

PERSONAL DATA

Personal data, such as height, weight, date and place of birth, and marital status were formerly standard items on a résumé. Now they are usually omitted.

It is appropriate to include a few informal statements about your travel experiences, hobbies, and interests, but do this only if you have extra space to fill.

Equal employment opportunity regulations require that employers recruit and hire in a nondiscriminatory manner, without regard to race, handicap, religion, color, sex, age, or national origin, and such information is now considered to have no bearing on a person's ability to do a job. Some job seekers combine interests and personal data under the headings Personal or Background Information and include such items as hobbies, travel, or unusual childhood experiences. But, unless you believe this information truly enhances your qualifications or you need to fill up the page, these topics are probably best left off your résumé.

REFERENCES

The names of references can be given along with their professional titles, addresses, and phone numbers if those involved have given you permission to use this information. If you have letters on file at your college or university, you may state on the résumé, "Placement dossier, including letters of recommendation, available from ———," giving the name of the appropriate university office. "References available upon request" may also be added to the end of the résumé, but since employers will request them if they are needed, the phrase is superfluous and may be omitted to save space.

To save space on your résumé and, perhaps more important, to give yourself greater flexibility and greater control over your references, you can develop and distribute several different lists of references, printed on separate sheets. You can create individualized lists for different job targets, and you can change the references as you meet more people who can assist you.

You should be aware that there is a difference between references and recommendations. References are provided by people who can tell potential employers about your background and how you might perform on the job. These individuals may be past employers, teachers, and others who have known you in academic settings, as well as persons who know you in a personal context. Recommendations, better stated as letters of recommendation, are written documents that tell potential employers about your background and capabilities. Whether you ask people to write letters of recommendation or simply to serve as references, you should be sure to keep them informed of your job-search activities. Those who write references for you should be active participants in the job search rather than names on a list or signatures on a letter. If they know what you are looking for and what

Whether you ask people to write letters of recommendation or simply to serve as references, you should be sure to keep them informed of your job-search activities.

efforts you have made, they can suggest potential employers and uncover job leads for you.

Under the *Family Educational Rights and Privacy Act* of 1974—referred to by some as "the Buckley Amendment" because James Buckley, a senator from New York, authored portions of the legislation—students are entitled to read letters of recommendation in their placement files unless they waive their right of access. The issue of whether you should waive your right of access, creating a completely "confidential" recommendation, is one that has been debated since the creation of the law in 1974. I do not believe that this is an issue the student job seeker should be concerned with. It should not matter to an employer whether you have read your letters of recommendation or not. What should matter is whether you have the qualifications to perform the tasks associated with the job you are applying for. Most employers rely much more on their own judgments of your qualifications than on the judgments of persons who have written recommendations. You should not be asking anyone to write a recommendation if there is a possibility they might write something that questions your capabilities. If you prepare your references by providing them a copy of your résumé and by sharing with them your goals and your own analysis of your qualifications for particular types of jobs, you should have nothing to worry about.

In addition, you should always request copies of letters of recommendation. If you receive copies, you can then waive your right of access and still know what appears in your file or you can maintain your right of access, depending on your personal opinions concerning this issue. If someone refuses to provide you with a copy, you should explore the reasons why and perhaps withdraw your request for a letter of recommendation or maintain your right of access to that particular letter.

Most employers rely much more on their own judgments of your qualifications than on the judgments of persons who have written recommendations.

Résumé Formats

There are three basic résumé formats—chronological, functional, and combination.

CHRONOLOGICAL

The chronological résumé presents information in reverse chronological order under major headings such as the traditional ones discussed above. This is the most common type of résumé and the easiest to develop because it simply lists experiences in the order in which they happened.

FUNCTIONAL

The functional résumé presents information under skills headings like those mentioned in the discussion of "Special Categories" above. Abilities and experiences are grouped according to job-related functions, such as research, statistical analysis, or supervision. This kind of résumé can be more work to write, but it can also be very effective for liberal arts job seekers who want to highlight skills that can be transferred from one field of endeavor to another. This format can be used successfully by recent graduates as well as by those re-entering the job market or changing career fields.

COMBINATION

The combination résumé represents a mix of the chronological and functional approaches, presenting some information under traditional headings and organizing other elements according to job functions.

All three formats can be used effectively by liberal arts job seekers. I would like to emphasize, however, that for most people it is a good idea to incorporate some type of functional component in the résumé. Liberal arts job seekers who think and speak in terms of skills usually have the most success. Unless you have a great deal of experience directly related to the job you want (in which case your work experience will speak for itself), you should either use skills headings or include a Summary of Skills or Qualifications section. By doing so, you present potential employers with the conclusions you want them to reach. This is better than leaving the interpretation of your abilities to chance.

Grant Bogle, District Manager for American Critical Care, screens numerous job applications each year, and he concurs with this view: "After reading traditional chronological résumés, I often find myself asking, 'What skills does this person possess?' Many times students have done a great deal—in the classroom, at work, and elsewhere—and have developed some very marketable skills through these experiences. However, if they do not list their skills for me, they leave it up to me to identify them. What if I miss their most important skills in the interview or in a quick reading of the résumé?"

You may, of course, decide against a functional résumé or even against a combination résumé. After examining some of the sample résumés on pages 34 to 86 you may decide that a chronological approach is also best for you. If you do not incorporate a functional component in your résumé, however, you should at least prepare a functional worksheet for yourself to help you assess your skills and prepare for interviews.

By including Skills Headings on your résumé, you present potential employers with the conclusions you want them to reach.

Remember that whatever format you choose, your résumé must be organized so that potential employers can locate information quickly. If you create a functional résumé, make sure it is well organized and has in some way identified your job titles and the organizations you have worked for, as well as your extracurricular offices and the organizations you have belonged to, and that the skills headings are appropriate to the jobs you are seeking. If you create a chronological résumé, be selective in the items you include so that they too are appropriate for your goals. If you create a combination résumé, make sure the functional section presents your qualifications in the most dynamic way possible and illustrates your ability to analyze your greatest strengths. Whatever the approach, your résumé must project your performance power!

TARGETED RÉSUMÉS vs. MULTIPURPOSE RÉSUMÉS

After you have decided which of the three basic formats to use, you should then think about whether your needs would be best served by a targeted résumé or a multipurpose résumé. Targeted résumés contain a statement of the job seeker's objective and present information in a way that supports that objective. Multipurpose résumés, on the other hand, include no specific statement of objective, and they can therefore be presented to potential employers in a number of different fields.

If at all possible, I suggest that you develop a targeted résumé. Résumés with statements of objective and supporting functional sections are very effective. If you have not decided on a single objective, you can develop more than one résumé, or you can develop a very well written multipurpose résumé. If you choose to write a multipurpose résumé, you must be sure to explain your goals and qualifications in the covering letters you write to potential employers. Some of the analyses in this book explain how you can add such documents as a Summary of Qualifications or a Skills Summary to a multipurpose résumé in order to orient it toward a particular kind of job. You may wish to develop one multipurpose résumé and several supplementary pages, one for each objective.

I believe it is wise, however, to limit yourself to three résumés, or, if you decide on a multipurpose résumé, three supplementary pages. You should be able to limit yourself to three major job targets. In fact, more than this at a given time is too much for most job seekers to handle. You do not want to suffer the embarrassment of sending

It is best to limit yourself to three major job targets and, at most, three different résumés.

the wrong résumé to an employer, and keep in mind that the cost of developing a good-looking résumé can be substantial.

LENGTH

I do not accept the myth of the one-page résumé. Your résumé should be as concise as possible, but it must communicate essential information. Do not limit yourself to an arbitrary length of one page before you have written it. If you have honed it down, edited out unnecessary information, and it is still longer than one page—fine! Employers read information that is organized and well presented. If your résumé turns out to be longer than a page, just make sure that the first page contains the most important information. Make the employer want to read the second page.

If your résumé is longer than one page, make sure that the first page contains the most important information.

Writing Your Rough Draft

The first thing you have to do before you begin to write is decide whether you will be developing a targeted résumé or a multipurpose résumé. If you have chosen to write a targeted résumé, first write down your job objective, referring to your Job Target Chart and your list of three first-choice jobs. Even if you opt not to include an employment objective, your résumé must show potential employers that you are familiar with your own capabilities and qualifications. Knowledge of self and knowledge of job functions are the keys to a successful liberal arts job search, and your résumé must reflect this knowledge if it is going to work for you.

Next review the discussions of résumé contents (page 87) and formats (page 92) and refer to the sample résumés you judged appropriate for your purposes in order to determine which format and headings you will use. Then make a list of the headings you think you will want to include. If you decide to use a chronological format, review your Chronological Flowchart and, using a felt-tip highlighter or circling with a pen or pencil, mark the entries you wish to include on your résumé. If you decide to write a functional résumé, review your Skills Flowchart to identify which skills you will feature and to decide under which headings they should appear.

You should now be ready to write your first draft. Don't be concerned at all about appearance or length at this point. Continually refer to

State your accomplishments clearly and with conviction. Don't be modest. This is your chance to brag.

your flowcharts and your Job Target Chart and base your entries on the items you highlighted as being the most important.

Write as freely and as quickly as you can, and refrain from being overly critical at this point. Include everything you think you might want to appear in the final draft. (You will probably be surprised to find that your rough draft ends up being several pages long!) The more comprehensive your rough draft is, the more effective your final draft will be. Use a format you like, but do not worry too much about the placement of headings or about highlighting techniques. Once your first draft is written, you will be able to relax and edit it and think about ways to improve the layout.

When describing academic, extracurricular, and employment experiences, be as thorough and descriptive as possible. Use active, skills-oriented phrasing. Refer to the list of appropriate action words and phrases below for suggestions.

When describing experiences, cite specific accomplishments and don't be modest. This is your chance to brag. If a fraternity or sorority fund-raising drive you chaired raised the most money of all campus organizations, say so. In fact, it's even a good idea to state exactly how much money was raised. If you figured out a way to effectively promote and sell certain items in a store you worked in, include that. State your accomplishments clearly and with conviction. Be proud of what you have done.

Don't feel that you have to use complete sentences in all sections. It's perfectly acceptable to use "telegram style," omitting articles and pronouns, especially first-person pronouns, which do not add to the clarity of descriptions. The phrasing should make sense, but it should also be as succinct as possible.

ACTION WORDS AND PHRASES

accommodated	advised	assisted
achieved	advocated	assumed
acquainted	altered	attached
activated	analyzed	attained
adapted	appraised	augmented
administered	approved	authorized
advertised	assembled	

analyzed procedures to assess their efficiency
analyzed ideas and situations from different perspectives
applied research data to develop proposals or reach
  conclusions
applied theory and abstract concepts to work settings
applied appropriate resources to problem-solving strategies

assessed needs of organization and implemented
  improvements

balanced	communicated	controlled
built	conceived	converted
classified	condensed	coordinated
collected	conferred	counseled
combined	consolidated	created
commanded	consulted	curtailed

created innovative solutions to problems
compiled, organized, and analyzed data
conveyed a positive image to the public

demonstrated	developed	discovered
designated	directed	dispatched
designed	disclosed	displayed
determined	discontinued	distributed

delegated responsibility to others for completion of tasks
defined parameters of problem situations
described events or objects accurately
designed experiments or research procedures
demonstrated appropriate assertiveness in various settings
  and circumstances

economized	evaluated	familiarized
educated	examined	formulated
eliminated	exchanged	governed
employed	executed	grouped
encouraged	expanded	guaranteed
established	expedited	guided
estimated	extended	

evaluated information and presented analyses
expressed opinions and preferences without offending
  others
formulated questions to clarify problems or to assess
  attitudes
generated trust and confidence of others

illustrated	initiated	inventoried
improved	instructed	invested
increased	interpreted	investigated
informed	introduced	lectured

identified alternative courses of action and strategies
identified information for specific situations and needs
identified critical issues to make decisions or solve problems
listened with objectivity and utilized information for
  problem solving

maintained	motivated	planned
managed	observed	prescribed
measured	obtained	procured
merged	operated	produced
minimized	organized	publicized
modernized	originated	published
modified		

managed time and resources effectively
motivated and managed personnel

marketed self, a product, or a service
organized people and material to achieve goals

recommended	simplified	terminated
rectified	solved	trained
reduced	sponsored	transferred
regulated	stabilized	transformed
removed	strengthened	unified
reorganized	studied	updated
repaired	supervised	utilized
replaced	supplemented	vetoed
reported	surpassed	wrote
restored	taught	

suggested possible long-range and short-range outcomes of
   actions
wrote effective promotional materials and designed
   advertising brochures

CRITIQUING YOUR ROUGH DRAFT

Now that your rough draft is completed, use the Critiquing Guidelines that appear below to judge the quality of the draft, make appropriate changes, and eventually develop the typed draft of your résumé.

At this stage, you should be more concerned about writing style and graphics. Review the sample résumés to identify phrasing, highlighting techniques, and layouts that suit your purposes. Use a dictionary to find the correct spelling of words that you are not sure of. The next draft should be as close to the final draft in content and format as possible, so this critiquing stage is very important.

Once you've worked through several revisions and *before* you have your résumé typeset and duplicated, ask a few people to critique your final version. Friends, family members, and former employers are good choices; they should all be able to tell you if you've left out something significant. Career counselors, placement officers, and other professionals who look at résumés all the time are also bound to have a lot of good, constructive advice.

After you've considered everyone's comments, incorporated some of their suggestions, and decided on your final version, proofread your résumé very thoroughly. Then have five of your friends proofread it, and then before you hand it over to the printer, proof it again. Your résumé *must* be error-free. If you find that it has a typographical error, a dangling phrase, an incomplete correction, or a stray mark of any kind, retype it, or, if it's already been typeset, have it redone. It's better to invest the extra money to have your résumé corrected than to use a résumé that presents you as a person who does not pay attention to detail.

Friends, family members, and former employers should all be able to tell you if you've left out something significant.

CRITIQUING GUIDELINES

Review the following questions to judge your résumé's quality and effectiveness. You should answer "yes" to each question. If you cannot do so, examine your rough draft carefully and make changes that will allow you to answer affirmatively. If completing your first critiquing, ignore questions that make reference to a final draft.

APPEARANCE

Is it neat and easy to read?

Do topic headings stand out?

Have you used space to highlight headings and important information?

Have you used underlining, CAPITALIZATION, shadow typing, varied type styles, and spacing to highlight important information?

Were you consistent in placement of headings and content—centered, margined, indented?

Have you used the best type style, or styles, to create the image you want?

Is your résumé free of typographical errors, misspelled words, messy erasures?

Does your résumé look professional and businesslike?

Is your final draft clear and dark enough for good duplication?

CONTENTS

Identifying information

Does your name stand out?

Are your address and phone number easy to find?

If more than one address or phone number appears, is it clear when each is to be used?

Objective statement

If it appears, does it project knowledge of the desired career field by using appropriate phrasing?

Does it stress job titles, job functions, your skills, or a combination of these?

Have you considered developing a multipurpose résumé without an objective, as well as one or more résumés with objectives?

Education

Have you presented school(s), degree(s), area(s) of concentration, courses, honors?

If an objective is stated, have you highlighted academic experiences that are most relevant?

Are grades or grade point averages presented, if complimentary?

Have you presented academic-related information appropriate for your goals?

Experience

Have you included all experiences that project skills and accomplishments?

Did you describe experiences in active phrasing, using skills-oriented and functionally descriptive words?

Did you discuss achievements and accomplishments, noting facts and figures when appropriate?

Are experiences grouped according to topics that are related to your goals or stated objective?

Have you really thought about all of the activities, paid and volunteer, that contributed to your developing the skills and abilities you possess?

Do job titles, organizations, or both, stand out as well as you desire? Could they be easily found by a potential employer?

Have you presented experiences in reverse chronological order? If not, is there logic behind the presentation?

Have you included dates with your descriptions? If not, do you have a good reason for leaving them out?

Extracurricular and community activities

Have you listed appropriate activities, noting leadership positions and describing responsibilities?

If you included organizations that might be controversial, have you considered how a potential employer might react?

Have you presented activities in clear fashion, avoiding acronyms and describing little-known organizations and awards?

Skills

Have you presented your skills in the language of potential employers, in terminology appropriate to your goals?

Have you been objective and thorough in your self-assessment, presenting skills you truly possess and those you feel confident using on the job?

Have you provided evidence concerning where you developed and utilized these skills, referring to experiences, education, or activities?

Qualifications summary

Have you outlined the qualifications you possess, those that would be attractive to an employer considering you for a position related to your objective?

Do you demonstrate an understanding of the target career field by using appropriate terminology and stressing appropriate characteristics?

Have you considered using headings such as Languages, Publications, or Related Experience to highlight important information?

Interests

Have you included only positive information, leaving out anything that can be viewed negatively, hurting your chances?

Personal data

If presented, did you leave out any information that could be used to discriminate against you?

References

If you listed references on your résumé, did you include name, title, organization, address, and phone number for each reference?

Did you present a statement concerning availability of references or supplemental materials? Have you made sure that your references will be readily available?

If you developed a separate list of references, matching your résumé, did you list name, title, organization, and phone number for each reference?

ORDER OF ELEMENTS

Are the most important topics first?

If your résumé is more than one page, is the most important information on the first page?

If you have developed more than one résumé, have you considered the order of appearance for each?

OVERALL PRESENTATION

Is your résumé well organized, presenting a professional image, highlighting the most important information?

Can you elaborate upon all elements of your résumé if called upon to do so in an interview?

Does your résumé present your qualifications in the best light possible, stressing skills?

Does your résumé make it easy for a potential employer to say "yes" to a request for an interview?

Is your résumé concise and thorough?

Is your résumé the most professional presentation of your ability to complete a task effectively and successfully?

Would you be proud to show a potential employer your résumé?

Production Techniques

Résumés can be typed or professionally typeset, or they can be produced by word processing. They can be traditional—laid out on standard 8 1/2-by-11-inch white paper—or innovative, with designs that incorporate various graphic techniques and make use of unusual paper sizes. What is important is that you realize that you are in control of the résumé-writing process. There is no one right way to produce a résumé, and you must decide on the contents and format that will suit you best.

The information on your Chronological Flowchart, Skills Flowchart, and Job Target Chart helped you decide what to include on your résumé and how to present it, and the sample résumés showed you how a number of job seekers sold their liberal arts power through an effective use of certain topics and formats. If you're still uncertain about how to design your résumé, reread the analyses that accompany each résumé to learn why specific categories appear and why a particular format was chosen.

As the sample résumés illustrate, you can achieve excellent results with either typing or typesetting. The two most important factors to keep in mind are the quality of the final typed document and the cost.

The two most important factors to keep in mind are the quality of the final typed document and the cost.

TYPING

If you are going to type your résumé, you must do so using a high-quality electronic business typewriter. Do not use a portable or manual model; the poor quality will show up in the duplicated copies. The better the typewriter, the crisper the finished version.

Some typewriters come equipped with various typing elements or "daisywheels" that enable you to use different type styles such as italic or boldface for highlighting purposes. These kinds of typewriters (IBM Selectric is one of the many brands that have this capability) can be rented for approximately $50 to $70 a month.

Instead of typing your résumé yourself, you may want to have it typed. Before agreeing to anything, however, ask to see a sample of the typist's work as well as samples of the various typing styles available. The cost of having a résumé professionally typed varies, ranging from $7 to $10 per page.

Having your résumé typeset can be one way of condensing it if you need to; a page-and-a-half of typewritten copy can easily be reduced to one page.

TYPESETTING

Typesetting is the process of setting copy in type, usually so that it can be printed on a press, as is done with books. Using this method can result in a very professional and distinctive-looking résumé, and it gives you the option of choosing from a wide variety of typefaces for headings and text. Résumés that are typeset can make an impression of creativity or conservatism, depending on the type style and layout.

Typesetting can be an expensive process, though, ranging in price from $25 to $35 per type-set page, duplication costs not included. If you can locate someone to typeset your résumé at an affordable price, you should consider this approach very seriously. If the costs of typesetting are prohibitive, then a good-quality typed version is the way to go.

One important thing to keep in mind, however, is that having your résumé typeset can be one way of condensing it if you need to; a page-and-a-half of typewritten copy can be reduced to one page or less, depending on the typeface used. The difference in cost between duplicating a one-page résumé and a two-page résumé might make typesetting a more attractive option.

RUB-ONS

You may wish to consider a cost-saving alternative to typesetting. This involves the use of rub-on lettering for major headings and a typewriter for the contents under the headings. Samples of résumés that illustrate this approach appear in Part 3. With a little practice, you can use these rub-on letters to create some very effective highlighting and some very striking résumés.

WORD PROCESSING

The word processor is a typewriter with a memory. When a résumé is typed—entered—on a word processor, the finished version is stored on tape or on a disk and is then retrievable at any time. To duplicate your résumé, you simply locate the résumé on the storage tape or disk and instruct the machine to print.

More and more students today have access to word-processing equipment that is hooked up to college and university computer facilities, and given the fact that you can make corrections easily and quickly and then store the latest version of your résumé indefinitely, it is an option you should definitely take advantage of. You can change objective statements as needed and rework the format and layout of your résumé in minutes. You might also be able to use your school's word-processing equipment to print your résumé. You should make sure, however, that the system you are using is equipped with a letter-quality daisywheel or impact printer; documents produced on dot-matrix printers are not really acceptable for business correspondence.

Some word processors have various typing elements or daisywheels that make it possible to change type styles; others have built-in shadow-printing capabilities, which makes it possible to highlight important words or headings. Keep this in mind when trying to decide whether to use word-processing equipment to duplicate your résumé.

PRINTING PHOTO-OFFSET vs. PHOTOCOPYING

Photo-offset is a printing process that involves making a photographic negative of the camera-ready copy, which can be either typed or typeset. The negative is made into a plate that is then used on a printing press.

Photocopying is a process of duplicating by means of a wet or dry chemical transfer. Almost all of us are accustomed to using photocopiers.

A few years ago I strongly recommended that all job seekers have their résumés printed by the photo-offset process. Now, although I still recommend offset printing, I do suggest that résumé writers explore the option of photocopying. Because offset printing is a true printing process it creates a very crisp duplication. Advances in photocopying equipment have made it possible to produce copies that are indistinguishable from printed versions, but not all photocopying services have the proper equipment. Photocopying can result in copies that have toner residue, with shadows or spots appearing on résumés.

Do NOT use a coin-operated photocopier like the ones you use in a library to duplicate your résumé. The paper in these machines is not high quality and your résumé will not create a very positive impression. NEVER use a wet paper copier, with slick chemical paper, to duplicate your résumé. Before you decide on a photo-offset or photocopying service, ask to see samples of work they have done. Photocopy services can immediately show you how your résumé will turn out. If you judge the quality of the photocopy acceptable—clean and crisp—you may wish to use this technique because it is usually much quicker and less expensive.

Photo-offset copying varies in cost, from $5 to $20 for a hundred copies of a one-page résumé, so it is important that you shop around for the best prices. The price of offset and photocopying will be influenced by the type of paper your résumé

You MUST have your résumé printed on high-quality bond paper.

is printed on. You must have your résumé printed on high-quality bond paper. Use a bond with some cotton fiber and texture. Photocopying on good-quality paper will range from 5¢ to 15¢ per page, thus a hundred copies of a one-page photocopied résumé would be $5 to $15. Sometimes offset printing is more expensive and other times photocopying is more expensive. You must get price estimates before selecting a duplication service.

Unless you have access to a word processor, it is suggested that you not type an original résumé for each employer. You should be involved in too many other job search activities to make this feasible. Employers understand that résumés are duplicated, but they do expect the duplication to be of the best quality.

Distribute copies of your résumé to as many people as possible. You will never be an effective job hunter if you are too possessive of your résumé.

HOW MANY COPIES SHOULD YOU HAVE?

It is better to have too many copies than too few. I suggest you have at least 50 copies of your résumé, even if you have more than one résumé, and that you obtain an estimate on the cost of 100 copies. As discussed earlier, the résumé is your way of initiating and maintaining communications with potential employers and resource persons as well as a tool to use throughout the interview process. Having 50 to 100 résumés on hand will mean that you'll always be ready to take advantage of a new opportunity. You should distribute your résumé to as many people as possible. You will never be an effective job hunter if you are too possessive of your résumé.

PAPER

Whether photocopied or photo-offset printed, your résumé must be duplicated on high-quality bond paper. Choose a conservative businesslike color; white, ivory, or off-white are perhaps the best. Beige or gray may be appropriate for more creative résumés or for contacting nontraditional employers, but bright colors should be avoided. The content of your résumé and covering letters, not the color of the paper they are printed on, is what needs to stand out. Again, do not duplicate your résumé on plain paper from a photocopier and avoid parchment-like erasable paper.

It is a good idea to purchase blank pages and envelopes of the same paper your résumé is printed on to use for covering letters and additional correspondence. Some job seekers have stationery printed to match their résumé, with the same type used for name and address. The total presentation of the résumé, stationery, and envelope as a matching set projects a strong, positive image.

DO SOME COMPARISON SHOPPING, THEN DECIDE

As you can tell from the previous discussion, the cost of developing a finished version and of duplicating a résumé will vary from technique to technique, and the range of possible costs is quite wide. I strongly suggest that you get estimates from at least three duplication or printing services before you make a final choice. Consult the Yellow Pages and contact the career planning and placement office of your school for suggestions. Some career planning and placement facilities are able to recommend typists, typesetters, and printers. Also ask for advice from counselors and others who have already completed their résumés.

SOME WAYS TO SAVE MONEY

Some colleges and universities have good-quality typewriters available for use by students. Ask around and locate one. If you can type your own finished version—without errors—you will save some money. Sometimes clerical staff persons want to earn a little extra money by typing résumés. These people may charge less than professional typists.

Some school newspapers have typesetting equipment. Ask if you can use this equipment or if you can have your résumé typeset for a minimal charge. If you have a friend who works for the newspaper, you might be able to have your résumé typeset for the price of a lunch or dinner.

More and more college and university computer centers make word-processing equipment available to students. You may use this equipment to develop a finished version or to duplicate your résumé, as well as to write covering letters to potential employers. If you use a word processor to duplicate your résumé, you will have to purchase paper. This can be done through printers, stationery stores, or printing suppliers. Shop around to get the best price on paper, and don't forget envelopes.

Even if you are not using a word processor, you may wish to purchase your own paper. You may find that you can get good-quality bond paper for less than a duplication service would charge. If you are thinking about buying your own paper, obtain estimates of what photocopying and photo-offset printing would cost if you supplied the paper. The cost of duplicating your résumé could be significantly lower if you provide the paper.

The cost of duplicating your résumé could be significantly lower if you provide the paper.

College and university printing offices—not frequently used by students, but often available to them—sometimes have excellent prices for students. Explore this option.

The key to saving money is doing preliminary research. Take the extra time to shop around and be an informed consumer.

Covering Letters

When you are making initial contact with a potential employer by mail, your résumé MUST be accompanied by a covering letter. There is simply no excuse for not sending one. Many employers report that they won't even look at a résumé that comes without at least a few lines of explanation.

Résumés can only tell potential employers what you have done. Covering letters can tell them why you became involved in particular activities, what you gained from the experiences, and, more importantly, why you are writing to them and what it is about your résumé that they should pay particular attention to. Covering letters allow you to cite accomplishments that would be of special interest to a given employer and to elaborate on specific sections of your résumé. Time and time again I am told by recruiters that covering letters are just as important as résumés when applicants are making initial contact by mail. Covering letters can in many cases determine whether you are granted an interview. Even if you plan to contact a potential employer by phone, send a covering letter first to present your background and questions and to prepare the employer for your call.

The sample covering letters on pages 110 to 116 are NOT meant to be copied word for word. Any correspondence with a potential employer must be yours; it must project your writing style and personality. The samples are meant to guide and motivate you as you undertake your own job-search actions. They illustrate various approaches that liberal arts job seekers may take when making initial contact with employers. (Refer back to Joseph E. Byrne's résumé on page 37 to better understand how his covering letters advance his interests.)

Covering letters may function as letters of inquiry when you are contacting potential employers to determine the hiring needs of an organization or as letters of application when you are responding to specific job advertisements. Covering letters should be used to

- Introduce yourself and to present your reasons for contacting the employer

- Draw attention to your résumé and to highlight specific qualifications

- Inform the employer that you will be contacting him or her soon

Covering letters are just as important as résumés when applicants are making initial contact by mail.

Everything a potential employer receives from you must project professionalism and your power to perform.

- Request information from someone who works in a field you are interested in.

There are several accepted formats for business correspondence, and covering letters should be written using one of them. The illustration of the components of a covering letter on page 110 shows one of the several standard styles.

Covering letters should always be addressed to the person who is responsible for initiating the review process or for making the ultimate hiring decision. Avoid sending your letters to "To Whom It May Concern," "Dear Sir or Madam," or "Personnel Director." Make a phone call or two to find out the name and title of the individual you should contact and to confirm the address of the hiring organization. Your placement office may also have current names of personnel officers.

The covering letter, like the résumé, is a sample of the work you can do for your next employer. Pay close attention to style and format. All correspondence with a potential employer should be typed on good-quality paper and be free of errors and erasures. Everything a potential employer receives from you—résumé, covering letter, follow-up letters—must project professionalism and your power to perform!

Your Street Address
City, State   Zip Code

The Date

[Space down four spaces.]

Ms. Betty Wilson
Director
Recruiting and Staffing
Jefferson Industries, Inc.
9463 East Broad Street
Richmond, Virginia 23261

Dear Ms. Wilson,

The opening paragraph should state why you are writing and why you are interested in the organization. If you are writing a letter of application, you should name the position for which you are applying and tell the employer how you became aware of it. A letter of inquiry should provide evidence of your career-mindedness; it helps to refer to specific job functions, if not titles. If you were referred to the employer by someone such as a career counselor, a former employer, or an aunt, this is also the best place to mention that person's name and to point out that he or she suggested you write.

The middle paragraph is where you draw attention to your résumé and highlight specific skills relevant to the potential employer. Present your motives for seeking employment with this organization and cite achievements and qualifications related to the position desired. If you have qualifications that are not noted on your résumé, this is your opportunity to discuss them.

The closing paragraph states what you will do next (such as calling to arrange an interview at the employer's convenience) or what you would like the recipient of the letter to do next. An assertive statement explaining what you plan to do and what you hope the employer will do is harder to ignore than a vague request for consideration.

Sincerely,

[Signature Here]

Your Name Typed

Enclosure [This indicates that your résumé or additional materials are enclosed.]

A pre-interview letter: This letter can be used to contact an on-campus recruiter in order to initiate interest prior to the campus visit. It can also be used to arrange a special interview if the recruiter's schedule is filled. An advance letter shows sales initiative and gives the recruiter a bit more time to judge an applicant's qualifications.

3877 University
Austin, Texas 78712
September 17, 1984

Mr. Lawrence Brooks
Manager
Corporate Recruiting
Procter & Gamble
P.O. Box 836
Cincinnati, Ohio 45201

Dear Mr. Brooks,

I am looking forward to your visit to the University of Texas at the beginning of next month. As I told you this morning on the phone, I will be graduating from UT this May and would very much like to work for Procter & Gamble as a Field Sales Representative.

My greatest strengths are in marketing ideas and services. Through a number of employment and extracurricular experiences I have gained a great deal of experience organizing, promoting, and publicizing events. I know I can sell and provide the sales support required of professional Field Sales Representatives. If by some chance I am unable to schedule an interview with you through our placement office, I will give you a call while you are on campus to see if we can get together to discuss my qualifications at a convenient time.

I am very interested in Procter & Gamble and sincerely hope that we can meet during your recruiting trip. Thank you for your consideration.

Sincerely,

Anne Marie Sonselle

Anne Marie Sonselle

Enclosure

3877 University
Austin, Texas 78712
March 25, 1985

Mr. Stephen P. Tatoe
Manager of College Relations
Frito-Lay
P.O. Box 741
Dallas, Texas 75235

Dear Mr. Tatoe,

I read the letter you recently sent to the Career Planning and Placement Office of the University of Texas College of Business Administration. I am writing to say that I would like to be considered for employment in Frito-Lay's marketing department. I will be graduating from the University of Texas this May, and I would very much like to begin a career in sales and marketing with your organization.

You will note from the enclosed résumé that many of my extracurricular and work experiences involved the organization, promotion, and publicizing of events. I have had direct sales experience soliciting potential customers for We Three Caterers and have been successful in managing employees in various capacities. Perhaps the most challenging and rewarding experience I have had to date was working with Congressman Gradison and the organizing committee of the University of Texas Literary Festival. I am confident that I have the sales and managerial skills required to be a contributing member of the Frito-Lay organization.

A letter and résumé can tell you only so much about my motivations and qualifications. I would welcome the opportunity to discuss my background with you in person and would travel to Dallas at my own expense to do so. I will call you at the end of next week to discuss whether such a meeting would be possible and to confirm appropriate next steps.

Thank you for your consideration.

Sincerely,

Anne Marie Sonselle

Anne Marie Sonselle

Enclosure

A letter of inquiry: By being creative and using an old newspaper want ad to uncover a potential job opening, Anne Marie might uncover a diamond in the rough.

3877 University
Austin, Texas 78712
April 1, 1985

Mrs. Carey Washington
Director of Personnel
Mattell Toys
3876 Rosecrans Avenue
Hawthorne, California 90250

Dear Mrs. Washington,

While reviewing past editions of the <u>Wall Street Journal</u>, I came across an advertisement you placed concerning an opening for a sales representative. I am sure that this particular post has been filled, but I am writing to ask whether another position has opened up since then.

Upon graduation from the University of Texas this May, I would like to begin a career in sales with an organization such as Mattell Toys. Many of my extracurricular and work experiences, detailed in the enclosed résumé, involved organizing, promoting, and publicizing events. I have had direct sales experience at We Three Caterers. Perhaps the most challenging and rewarding were my experiences with Congressman Gradison and the University of Texas Literary Festival. I know that I can sell, and I know that I am capable of providing the sales support required of successful sales representatives.

I look forward to hearing from you concerning possible opportunities. Thank you for your consideration.

Sincerely,

Anne Marie Sonselle

Anne Marie Sonselle

Enclosure

A request for an informational interview.

Box 1222
Tulane University
New Orleans, LA 70118
February 18, 1985

Mr. James L. Throser
Blane, Collier, and Phips
Suite 3987
One Shell Square
New Orleans, LA 70118

Dear Mr. Throser,

I am writing on the recommendation of Joan Webster, the Director of Career
Planning and Placement at Tulane University. Ms. Webster and I have
discussed my interest in the field of law, and she suggested that since you
are an alumnus of both Tulane University and the Tulane School of Law, you
might be willing to offer some advice and provide me with information about
the best ways to prepare for a career in law. I have enclosed a copy of my
résumé to familiarize you with my background.

At present I am looking for a position as a paralegal or legal assistant. It
is my intention to gain some exposure to legal work and learn some of the
fundamental skills required of a lawyer before applying to law school one or
two years down the road. I would be interested in your thoughts concerning
this strategy and, of course, would welcome any assistance or advice you
could provide.

I understand how busy you are, so I will come with specific questions about
the legal profession. I will call your office to arrange an appointment at
your convenience.

Thank you for your consideration.

Sincerely,

Joseph E. Byrne

Joseph E. Byrne

Enclosure

A letter of inquiry: Using a lead gained through an informational interview, Joseph writes to inquire about possible job openings.

Box 1222
Tulane University
New Orleans, LA 70118
March 12, 1985

Ms. Lane Brenden
Orin and Thayer
Suite 777
One Shell Square
New Orleans, LA 70118

Dear Ms. Brenden,

I am writing on the recommendation of James Throser of Blane, Collier, and Phips. Mr. Throser and I have discussed my interest in the legal profession and my current efforts to locate a law-related position.

As noted on the enclosed résumé, I would like to use my research and writing skills in a law office after graduating from Tulane in December. My courses have required me to undertake a great many research projects and write many papers. Enclosed you will find a few abstracts of my efforts. They are intended to illustrate my capacity to do research and report findings in appropriate formats. I understand that these are skills that are required of paralegals and legal assistants.

I work well under the pressure of deadlines and I am used to paying close attention to detail. I have had experience working as part of a team, and I have come to learn that one must work extremely hard in order to achieve success. I am willing and able to do so for Orin and Thayer.

Are there any openings for paralegals or legal assistants in your firm at the present time?

I will call you the week of March 18th to discuss employment opportunities with Orin and Thayer. Thank you very much for your consideration.

Sincerely,

Joseph E. Byrne

Joseph E. Byrne

Enclosures

A letter of application: Used to respond to a job posting, this letter highlights skills and motivation while demonstrating the applicant's ability to write a good business letter.

Box 1222
Tulane University
New Orleans, LA 70118
April 3, 1985

Ms. Marie Jeannette
Paralegal Manager
Daley, Daley, and Rogers
200 Park Avenue
New York, NY 10166

Dear Ms. Jeannette,

I am writing to apply for the paralegal position that was posted in the Tulane University Career Planning and Placement office. The position described in your posting seems to match my career goals and qualifications quite nicely.

As noted on the enclosed résumé, I would like to utilize my research and writing skills while working for a law firm as a paralegal. My academic courses have required a great many research projects and papers. Please find enclosed a few abstracts of my efforts. I hope they demonstrate to you my capacity to undertake research and report findings in a clear and concise fashion.

I can work well under the pressure of deadlines, and I have been involved in a great many group projects. My work experiences have taught me that one must be prepared to work beyond the typical forty-hour week to achieve success. I am willing and able to do so for Daley, Daley, and Rogers.

Your active consideration of my credentials would be greatly appreciated. I will call you next Friday to confirm receipt of this letter and to discuss appropriate next steps. Please feel free to contact me if you require additional information to support my candidacy.

Thank you.

Sincerely,

Joseph E. Byrne

Joseph E. Byrne

Enclosures

A Bibliography for Liberal Arts Majors

Aside From Teaching, What in the World Can You Do?, Dorothy K. Bestor, University of Washington Press, Seattle, Washington. A collection of essays dealing with career strategies for liberal arts graduates. The book presents material drawn from the author's experiences as a teacher and career counselor and from interviews and questionnaires dealing with liberal arts career issues. The extensive bibliography of career-related publications in this book should not be overlooked.

Catalyst Career Information, Catalyst, New York. This is a series of publications, including the "Career Options Series for Undergraduate Women," "Educational Opportunities Series," and "Career Opportunities Series," all of which deal with careers and job search strategies. Although the materials are directed toward women and published by a clearinghouse for information on careers for women, the information is applicable to men and women.

The Encyclopedia of Careers and Vocational Guidance, J. G. Ferguson Publishing Company, Chicago, Illinois. A two-volume publication providing a great deal of information on broad career areas and specific jobs within the areas. Volume I is composed of overviews of major industries and areas of work. Volume II contains articles on 220 specific occupational categories. The two are cross-referenced and designed to supplement each other.

The "Job Finders" series, Mainstream Access, Prentice-Hall, Englewood Cliffs, New Jersey. A collection of several books covering career fields such as banking, data processing/information technology, public relations, publishing, and others. Partial listings of potential employers in each field are contained in the books. Field-specific bibliographies appear at the end of each publication.

Jobs for English Majors and Other Smart People, John Munschauer, Peterson's Guides, Princeton, New Jersey. A publication dealing effectively with job search issues for English majors and other liberal arts graduates. It provides the information and motivation required to implement a successful job search.

The "Opportunities In" series, Vocational Manuals, Inc., Louisville, Kentucky. A series of books dealing with subject areas ranging from accounting to veterinary medicine. Liberal arts career researchers can find valuable information on over 60 fields.

The Occupational Outlook Handbook, U.S. Department of Labor, Washington, D.C. This reference book discusses occupations according to "clusters" of related jobs. The handbook is published about every two years and is a source of basic information about career fields. Each discussion follows a standard format, making comparisons of different fields easy.

The Dictionary of Occupational Titles, U.S. Department of Labor, Washington, D.C. This publication, a cousin of the Occupational Outlook Handbook, defines over 20,000 jobs according to a system that uses occupational code numbers to classify jobs by the type of work performed, training required, physical demands, and working conditions. The code system can be frustrating at first, but be patient with this publication. It's really a very good resource.

Directories and Periodicals. If you are researching potential career fields or trying to locate potential employers, make sure you check directories that index organizations by geographic and functional categories and periodicals that deal with subject areas you are interested in. Directories listing all of the advertising agencies, consulting firms, and public relations organizations in the United States and periodicals written for members of these career fields are available in most reference libraries.

Have You Seen These Other Publications from Peterson's Guides?

Summer Jobs:
Finding Them, Getting Them, Enjoying Them
Sandra Schocket

Designed especially for high school and college students, this valuable guide shows how to find and get good summer jobs. It covers topics such as the process of finding a summer job, specific fields of employment that have summer jobs for students, options for students who want nontraditional types of employment (volunteer work, internships, working abroad, self-employment), and additional resources that might aid students in their summer job search.

6" x 9", 170 pages   Stock no. 3258
ISBN 0-87866-325-8   **$5.95** paperback

Peterson's Annual Guides/Careers
Business and Management Jobs 1985
Editor: Christopher Billy

This distinctive new career guide details hundreds of organizations that recruit employees in the nontechnical areas of business and management. In addition to giving specific information about each employer, the book tells applicants how to match their academic background to specific openings.

8½" x 11", 226 pages   Stock no. 2499
ISBN 0-87866-249-9   **$12.95** paperback

Jobs for English Majors and Other Smart People
John L. Munschauer

This book recognizes the realities of the job market for the generalist, the inexperienced, the career changer. The author offers down-to-earth advice about such common concerns as when to send and when not to send a résumé, how to identify alternative careers, and how to create a job when there is no advertised opening.

5½" x 8½", 180 pages   Stock no. 1441
ISBN 0-87866-144-1   **$6.95** paperback

Finding a Job in Your Field:
A Handbook for Ph.D.'s and M.A.'s
Rebecca Anthony and Gerald Roe

This practical and thorough guide is the only book written especially for holders of advanced degrees to explain how they should prepare for academic and professional employment. It includes an assessment of the job choices available, advice on organizing a job search, tips on how to write effective vitas and résumés, advice on how to interview with search committees, and other specific and very helpful information.

6" x 9", 144 pages   Stock no. 2782
ISBN 0-87866-278-2   **$8.95** paperback

Who Offers Part-Time Degree Programs?
SECOND EDITION
Editor: Kim R. Kaye

The only handy reference book that covers part-time undergraduate and graduate degree programs offered by colleges and universities throughout the United States. It provides a complete, up-to-date overview of daytime, evening, weekend, summer, and external degree programs at more than 2,000 institutions.

7" x 9½", 417 pages   Stock no. 2855
ISBN 0-87866-285-5   **$7.95** paperback

New Horizons:
The Education and Career Guide for Adults
William C. Haponski, Ph.D., and Charles E. McCabe, M.B.A.

Covers a broad spectrum of options for adults who want to continue their education, including bachelor's and associate degree, external degree, and professional certificate programs, as well as correspondence courses. Originally published as *Back to School: The College Guide for Adults,* this new edition places heavier emphasis on career-related aspects of adult education. March 1985.

6" x 9", 250 pages (approx.)   Stock no. 3304
ISBN 0-87866-330-4   **$7.95** paperback

Where to Start:
An Annotated Career-planning Bibliography
FOURTH EDITION, 1983–85
Madeline T. Rockcastle

This book is published by Cornell University's Career Center, which houses one of the best career libraries in the nation, and describes the career-planning publications used there. It covers books, periodicals, audiovisual resources, and other materials and is an invaluable tool for human resource managers, counselors, and librarians in both corporate and academic organizations.

8½" x 11", 206 pages   Stock no. 6260
ISBN 0-87866-260-X   **$11.95** paperback

Peterson's Annual Guides/Undergraduate Study
Guide to Four-Year Colleges 1985
FIFTEENTH EDITION
Managing Editor: Kim R. Kaye
Book Editor: Joan H. Hunter

The largest, most up-to-date guide to all 1,900 accredited four-year colleges in the United States and Canada. Contains concise college profiles, a reader guidance section, and two-page "Messages from the Colleges" that are found in no other guide.

8½" x 11", 2,188 pages   Stock no. 2316
ISBN 0-87866-231-6   **$12.95** paperback

The Athlete's Game Plan for College and Career
Stephen Figler and Howard Figler

The first book to deal with *all* the commitments of a student athlete—academic achievement, athletic responsibilities, and career selection—and to show how to keep them in balance. Covers college selection, dealing with recruiters, financial aid, eligibility for college sports, study skills, coping strategies, education and athletics as bridges to career success, and job-hunting techniques.

6" x 9", 279 pages   Stock no. 2669
ISBN 0-87866-266-9   **$9.95** paperback

Peterson's Annual Guides/Graduate Study
Graduate and Professional Programs:
An Overview 1985
NINETEENTH EDITION
Series Editor: Diane Conley

Covers the whole spectrum of U.S. and Canadian graduate programs in a single reliable volume. A special table correlates over 1,350 schools with the graduate and professional degrees they offer.

8½" x 11", 885 pages   Stock no. 2340
ISBN 0-87866-234-0   **$15.95** paperback

The Independent Study Catalog:
NUCEA's Guide to Independent Study Through
Correspondence Instruction 1983–1985
Editor: Joan H. Hunter

A new edition of the ultimate education "wishbook" for people who want to study on their own without the restrictions of regular class attendance. Students can choose from more than 12,000 correspondence courses offered by 72 colleges and universities. Credit and noncredit courses are available at the elementary, high school, undergraduate, and graduate levels.

8½" x 11", 120 pages   Stock no. 1808
ISBN 0-87866-180-8   **$5.95** paperback

The College Money Handbook 1985:
The Complete Guide to Expenses, Scholarships,
Loans, Jobs, and Special Aid Programs at Four-Year
Colleges
SECOND EDITION
Editor: Karen C. Hegener

The only book that describes the complete picture of costs and financial aid at accredited four-year colleges in the United States. The book is divided into three sections: an overview of the financial aid process and ways to make it work for you; cost and aid profiles of each college, showing need-based and merit scholarship programs available; and directories listing colleges by the types of financial aid programs they offer.

8½" x 11", 531 pages   Stock no. 2820
ISBN 0-87866-282-0   **$12.95** paperback

How to Order

These publications are available from all good booksellers, or you may order direct from **Peterson's Guides, Dept. 5613, P.O. Box 2123, Princeton, New Jersey 08540.** Please note that prices are necessarily subject to change without notice.

- Enclose full payment for each book, plus postage and handling charges as follows:

Amount of Order	4th-Class Postage and Handling Charges
$1–$10	$1.25
$10.01–$20	$2.00
$20.01–$40	$3.00
$40.01 +	Add $1.00 shipping and handling for every additional $20 worth of books ordered.

Place your order TOLL-FREE by calling 800-225-0261 between 8:30 A.M. and 4:30 P.M. Eastern time, Monday through Friday. From New Jersey, Alaska, Hawaii, and outside the United States, call 609-924-5338. Telephone orders over $15 may be charged to your charge card; institutional and trade orders over $20 may be billed.

- For faster shipment via United Parcel Service (UPS), add $2.00 over and above the appropriate fourth-class book-rate charges listed.

- Bookstores and tax-exempt organizations should contact us for appropriate discounts.

- You may charge your order to VISA, MasterCard, or American Express. Minimum charge order: $15. Please include the name, account number, and validation and expiration dates for charge orders.

- New Jersey residents should add 6% sales tax to the cost of the books, excluding the postage and handling charge.

- Write for a free catalog describing all of our latest publications.